CHOSEN AND FLAWED

CHOSEN AND FLAWED

A BEHAVIORAL ANALYSIS OF BIBLICAL CHARACTERS

ARVINDER GINDA

Copyright © 2024 Emotional Intelligence LLC
All rights reserved.

FIRST EDITION

CHOSEN AND FLAWED
A Behavioral Analysis of Biblical Characters

ISBN 978-1-5445-4703-9 Hardcover
     978-1-5445-4702-2 Paperback
     978-1-5445-4704-6 Ebook

The views and opinions expressed in *Chosen and Flawed* are the author's alone and do not reflect the views of the FBI.

I am dedicating this book to all my teachers who have helped me along the way—from the little country school Nuestro Elementary to Sutter High School. To my first teacher and role model— my father, Dharam Pal Ginda—who was a teacher in India for nineteen years before moving to the United States. He gave up his dream of furthering his education and instead had to work as a migrant worker to better provide for his family. And to Mrs. Susan Young, who made sure I would go to college by helping me apply for scholarships and giving me a lifetime of encouragement. To Mrs. Johnson, Mrs. Stockton, Mr. Reid, Mr. Crowhurst, Mr. Robison, Coach Turner, Coach Baroni, Mr. Crabtree, and countless others who took the time to ensure that I learned English and enunciated my words clearly, and held me accountable to a higher learning. And to the many teachers currently in my life who are teaching me still, regardless of my age.

CONTENTS

FOREWORD xi

INTRODUCTION 1

Chapter 1
ADAM AND EVE 15
IN THE BEGINNING THERE WAS . . . EVE

Chapter 2
CAIN AND ABEL 27
NOT-SO-BROTHERLY LOVE

Chapter 3
NOAH 37
BEING A HERO CAN BE TRAUMATIC

Chapter 4
JOB 45
SUFFERING IN LOUD SILENCE

Chapter 5
ABRAHAM AND SARAH 59
A BETRAYAL OF IMPROBABLE PROPORTIONS

Chapter 6
HAGAR AND ISHMAEL 73
THE RESILIENCE OF A SINGLE MOTHER

Chapter 7
ISAAC 83
OBEDIENCE TO THE FATHER...
THE HEAVENLY FATHER

Chapter 8
JACOB AND ESAU 93
LIFE'S SCARS CAN BE DECEIVING

Chapter 9
JOSEPH 109
PURPOSE IN THE PAIN

Chapter 10
MOSES 127
FRUSTRATED DISOBEDIENCE WITH GOD'S LOVE

Chapter 11
SAMSON 143
IDLE MINDS CAN LEAD TO DARK TIMES

Chapter 12
DAVID 157
A FLAWED MAN, BUT A MAN AFTER GOD'S OWN HEART

Chapter 13
SOLOMON 171
TRUE WISDOM DOES NOT ALWAYS
AMOUNT TO TRANQUILITY

Chapter 14
ELIJAH 183
THE PROPHET WHO LOST HIS WILL TO LIVE
BUT NEVER DIED

Chapter 15
JONAH 197
FAILURE TO LAUNCH

Chapter 16
DANIEL 205
LIVING A LIFE WORTH DYING FOR

Chapter 17
ESTHER 217
AN UNDERCOVER AGENT FOR GOD

CONCLUSION 229
MESSAGE OF HOPE IN TIMES OF UNCERTAINTY

ACKNOWLEDGMENTS 237

ABOUT THE AUTHOR 239

FOREWORD

This book by Arvinder "Vinny" Ginda is a must-read.
Why?

I got to know Vinny when he became an FBI Crisis (hostage) Negotiator and I was assigned to CNU, the FBI Crisis Negotiation Unit at the Critical Incident Response Group, a headquarters division. CNU ran the program operationally, administered it, and did all the training for it. A hybrid operation normally in three separate places, we were a one-stop shop for the whole program.

Vinny stood out immediately not only for being talented and insightful, but also a really good guy.

I got to know him even further when he became a member of the CINT, the Critical Incident Negotiation Team, the FBI's top-tier Crisis Negotiators who are deployed from across the country when the "stuff" has really hit the fan. I was in charge of the FBI response and deployment of our Crisis Negotiators to any kidnapping of any American anywhere in the world.

It's a big world, and the incidence of Americans finding themselves kidnapped and in their darkest hour is not a rare occurrence. It's their family's darkest hour too. On any given day there are anywhere from one to four Americans directly facing this peril. I relied on Vinny for help in more than one tough situation and knew I could count on him anytime with no notice at all.

Vinny helped save lives.

Real practitioners of hostage/crisis negotiation, who are really good at it, are both spiritual and operational. They are also very entrepreneurial. This makes them great for tackling many of life's toughest challenges. It also often makes them very frustrating for bureaucrats lacking spiritual depth to deal with.

I never really knew where Vinny got those qualities...I just knew he had them.

Vinny's decency, spiritual curiosity, and intellectual insight come through in this book. It's a fascinating perspective on several of history's (and God's) most interesting entrepreneurs.

We (you and I) often wish our heroes weren't flawed. I did when I was younger and I probably still do. Yet I know this isn't the case. I love that Vinny took this approach in this book.

Read this book and go on this journey. Maybe you will take it a little easier on yourself and your neighbor as a result.

I wish you the best.

—CHRIS VOSS
Author of *Never Split the Difference:*
Negotiating as If Your Life Depended on It

INTRODUCTION

In ancient Chinese folklore, there is a tale of two pots—one flawless and the other cracked. The imperfect pot, aware of its limitations in carrying water compared to its companion, urges the villager to discard it. Convinced of its inadequacy, the cracked pot sees itself as unable to fulfill its purpose. However, the wise villager encourages the pot to reflect on the journey they have taken together every day. Along the path lie blossoming flowers that the pot has nurtured with the water it emanated during their travels. Despite its imperfections, the cracked pot has inadvertently created something truly beautiful.

Like the broken pot, we are all "chosen and flawed" in various areas of our lives. Oftentimes, we are too busy pointing out our own and others' flaws rather than searching for and defining the good that is in us. It is a product of the fallen nature of humanity that our thinking naturally trends toward negative thoughts. We have a propensity to think badly of ourselves and others—to judge. Strangely, it seems our brains have an easier time accepting the negative rather than the positive aspects of our lives. The beauty of being chosen and flawed is that the "chosen" part is what matters. We all have weaknesses and shortcomings, yet God chooses us regardless. If we can focus more on the "chosen" part of our existence, it can help us work through the aspects that are flawed, using them as instruments of good instead of evil, of blessing and healing rather than cursing and harming.

FROM A VILLAGE TO THE BRIGHT LIGHTS OF THE BIG CITY

My personal and professional lives have challenged me in ways I could never have imagined. At times, I felt I was "chosen" for my profession, as though it was exactly the right fit for me and there was really nothing else I could do or even wanted to do—likewise, for my family. There is a sense of rightness, a feeling of peace, a comforting certainty that you experience when you are where you should be and doing what you should be doing. Yet, I've also made mistakes and had my flaws exposed in both spheres of my life.

Some of my earliest childhood memories consist of me running around in my village in Punjab, India. I remember my mom and dad, along with my six siblings, all living in a small room with dirt floors and no electricity. I remember playing a game of marbles or gulli-danda (a game that involves using a large stick to hit a smaller tapered stick while it is airborne). I never really knew that we were poor at that age. I just understood it to be life during those early years. It really wasn't until we came to America on August 13, 1982—my eighth birthday—when we landed in San Francisco, that things changed. I remember specifically the thoughts that came racing into my head as I began to see people with different skin color or hair color. Everybody talked weird and sounded even funnier. I remember my first taste of chocolate and Pepsi and realizing how much I hated it because the tastes were overwhelming. Every aspect of life was different, from my language, family, and friends to even my living situation. We went from having no indoor plumbing or electricity to having a house with multiple rooms and a single black-and-white TV.

Being born a Hindu, I never really knew of any Western religions or their ideals. I first came to learn about Christianity when some of my dearest friends invited me to church in my early teen years.

And from there, the journey began. I came to believe in Christ at a church camp in the summer of 1990, and I was saved. I was the only member of my very traditional Hindu family who attended church and had converted to Christianity. It was the first time in my life that religion made sense. The fact that I could pray directly to one God, and I could talk to Him at any time, seemed quite simple. It brought a sense of peace and being accepted for who I was. Needless to say, that was not something anyone in my family or immediate circle of East Indian friends would accept easily. However, I remained steadfast in my faith and learned more and more about Jesus and the teachings in the Bible.

Coming to a country where I had to learn a new language and new way of life, and adapt to new cultural norms with the conflict of still attempting to hold onto my familial values, was not an easy task. Living at home with a very traditional family and then attending school with friends who did not look like me—and had very different upbringings—at times caused an identity crisis. I felt the further sting of this identity crisis when my Christian friends could not pronounce the name "Arvinder" and a fellow church member decided to give me the name "Vinny." Accepting the name and the identity attached to it was something, unfortunately, I could not talk to my family about.

As time went on, I got married, had kids, and had a career in local law enforcement and then the FBI. I did the best that I could, but I know I had many shortcomings. Somewhere along the way, I got lost in my own journey and allowed my pride, guilt, sense of entitlement, and shame to lead me down a path of self-destructive behavior. I made decisions that hurt my family, friends, and coworkers without considering the consequences of those decisions. Arrogance and a false perception of invincibility caused my world to begin to collapse around me. I know I was to blame for my own shortcomings, and I did not recognize that they were a plea for help.

Those unfortunate and painful times only got worse. My physical health began to deteriorate, and my career was on the verge of ending sooner than I had anticipated. I turned to my church only to face another proverbial door being slammed in my face. I began to question my relationship with God and asked why He would put my children through the hell they were going through. I began to question the teachings of my church because I could not agree with a system that diminished the role of women and children when in the eyes of God we are all to be treated equally. I began to feel more like an outsider and a wanderer than a church member.

This challenging time in my life altered my perspective on my personal and professional relationships. I had spent years and years cultivating connections with friends in a professional setting where I finally felt comfortable enough to allow people into my personal life. Once I began going through my hardships, all of those "close" friends were nowhere to be found. Not a single person checked in or called to see how I was or what I was going through. I felt like a pariah in a culture where I was once accepted. I felt alone even though I was in a room full of people. For once in my life, I felt broken, bruised, and invisible. Where I once felt invincible, I now felt at my lowest. An FBI Special Agent who had served two tours in Iraq and countless overseas missions in hostile environments with no fear of death—that strength, courage, identity, and invincibility was all stripped away. And I realized

I needed to figure out a way out of this mess of a life I had created. I no longer felt chosen for the greater good.

I had taught countless lessons on characters of the Bible who had failed over and over; despite their failures, God still had a plan for His broken children. I felt if I had a chance of surviving this junction in my life, it would only be through going back and analyzing not only my life but the lives of those others who were also broken and bruised. I wanted to further understand why some of our most important biblical heroes made the choices they made.

I took this journey in the hopes of learning that I am worthy of being accepted for my failures and flaws. And that I too can be chosen to do something worthwhile to serve God in the hopes that I can finally find what I'm looking for... some peace, joy, rest, and love.

When I started writing this book, I never considered I would be applying my skills doing the behavioral analysis of characters in the Bible. Most of my experience has been analyzing the behaviors of suspects, witnesses, victims, or various family members. My experience in the FBI and local law enforcement and my background in psychology have always inspired me to further my understanding of major aspects of human behavior. The question I am driven to answer is: why do people make the choices they make? I'm always trying to learn about motivations, needs, wants, desires, the behaviors that arise from them, and the underlying beliefs that inform and direct those behaviors. What propels the choices people make? Do we have a choice or is it compulsion?

Over the course of thirty years in law enforcement, I learned early on if I wanted to be successful in solving cases, I had to truly understand human behavior. What it always came down to was a process often referred to as behavioral analysis, which involves studying patterns of behavior to gain insight into an individual's thoughts, feelings, and motivations. Behavioral analysis also looks for consistent behaviors and deviations from the norm to understand the underlying factors influencing behavior.

Another key aspect that I took into consideration for these biblical characters was their emotional intelligence. Emotional intelligence is the ability to make rational decisions by controlling your emotions in order to increase your chances of success, while minimizing your margin of error, for better decision-making. Emotional intelligence also refers to the ability to recognize, understand, and manage one's own emotions as well as the emotions of others. This key aspect of emotionality also considers an individual's tone, pace, and pitch when they are speaking. The way things are said is oftentimes more important than what is said. When I analyze an individual's behavior, I have to consider all of these factors to develop the best possible assessment of their personality. This level of logical and strategic thinking allowed me to obtain numerous confessions in interrogations and build rapport with some of the most difficult individuals I encountered.

The people of the Bible are not just characters in a storybook. They were actual people who made more than a few mistakes. They made some huge errors of judgment and terrible choices with serious and long-lasting consequences. All of them sinned, and some of them went as far as committing crimes. Lies, betrayal, adultery, conspiracy, murder—you name it. Many of the biblical heroes acted like villains on occasion, but when we take a deeper look inside to explore their emotions and feelings and try to put ourselves in their shoes, we can learn from them.

HUMANIZING THE PAST

The problems and flaws we have today are the same ones we read about in the Bible. The world may have changed dramatically, but people haven't, nor have the underlying causes of all our troubles. Problems may manifest themselves in different forms, but the root of it all remains the same. We are fallen creatures, born sinful. However, we are also born convertible and teachable—born with the capacity to know God and to experience His comfort and His power despite our imperfections, to be used by Him regardless of our failings.

There are over three thousand people named in the Bible, and an analysis could be written on any of those individuals. In this particular book, I focus on characters not in the New Testament but rather on several individuals from the Old Testament: Adam and Eve, Cain and Abel, Noah, Job, Esther, Abraham, Moses, David, and Solomon. The stories are very familiar to many of us, but how much do we really know about these people and their lives? I wanted to lay the foundation of these characters as described in the Bible because of their familiarity with various cultures. Numerous individuals from the Old Testament are also referred to in the Hebrew Bible as well as the Koran.

One of the main driving forces in conducting this analysis of biblical characters is to humanize these figures whom we have heard and read about. I analyze the behavior of various well-known Bible figures with the goal of explaining their human reactions to the often supernatural events they experienced. For example, I wanted to understand what Noah must have felt as the Ark doors closed while people stood outside mocking him. Was Moses enabling the Israelites to be more dependent on him rather than God while they wandered the desert?

How did Jacob's emotional intelligence change when he met Rachel? How did Daniel feel when his own "coworkers" betrayed him and conspired to have him thrown into the lion's den even though he did nothing wrong? How was it that the wisest man alive, Solomon, could not find true love even though he had married over seven hundred wives? How did Elijah, a man who had such a strong relationship with God, develop such a deep level of depression that he lay down and just wanted to die? What is the untold story of Hagar, a slave woman who became Abraham's wife—but more importantly, became a strong, independent single mom who went on to raise a son who became a father of many nations in the Middle East? At the end of the day, I wanted to remember that our biblical heroes who have always been revered and honored were just people who made mistakes similar to the ones we make today. I wanted to explore the human side of these individuals rather than the songs of praise that are often sung about their unfathomable relationship with God.

COMMUNICATION, GOD'S GRACE, AND GOOD STEWARDSHIP

Through this analysis, I sought to understand these figures' behaviors, emotions, baselines, and decision-making capabilities in a state of crisis, as well as their overall emotional intelligence. One of the themes throughout the chapters of this book is communication breakdowns, and all of the aforementioned aspects have an impact on communication. The characters studied often failed to act in accordance with what God had promised them or instructed them to do. They also communicated improperly, unclearly, dishonestly, or inappropriately with others. Such failure to communicate clearly and effectively underpins almost all relationship problems. You and I have experienced that.

Effective communication starts with good listening. God does that well. We don't. As it does not come naturally, we must be taught the skill of active listening: giving your undivided attention, showing genuine interest, and being open to understanding different perspectives. Everyone's voice deserves to be heard and valued. Choose your words wisely. Words have immense power, so let's use them to uplift and inspire. Be mindful of your tone, speak kindly, and avoid negative language.

Effective communication is a skill that takes time to develop. Don't be discouraged by setbacks or misunderstandings. Instead, view them as opportunities for growth and learning. Embrace the journey, keep practicing, and watch your communication skills flourish. Remember, my friends, effective communication has the power to transform our relationships, both personal and professional.

Our God is perfect. He does not make mistakes, He does not say or do the wrong thing, He does not act impulsively, and He has never put his foot in His mouth. His attempts to speak with us, His children, have always been motivated by love and saturated in grace. We are the ones who get it wrong with each other and with God. There is no doubt God spoke to these individuals we will consider in a clear and concise way that could not be misunderstood. Once they received the message, oftentimes their actions and choices, both propelled and exposed by their flaws, led to major failures because they began to apply their own skewed perspectives rather than simply doing what God had wanted them to do.

God ultimately has a plan for all of us. Nothing happens just by chance; we exist in the place we are because we're supposed to be there for that moment—maybe to move ourselves on our own journey, or maybe to help someone else.

From the very beginning, God designed a plan for humanity to possess free will. This free will grants us the power to think, reason, and choose our own paths. However, with every choice made, there are inevitable consequences, whether positive or negative. God's intention has always been for us to align our purpose with His plan, rather than our own. Regrettably, this simple principle was disrupted by the serpent in the Garden of Eden, leading to lasting repercussions that continue to affect us today. Despite the challenges brought about by our ability to make choices, God continues to guide us toward being good stewards of our lives. This involves utilizing essential skills such as patience, empathy, compassion, and active listening in our interactions with others. By prioritizing a life lived for God, others, and finally ourselves, we can navigate the complexities of decision-making and consequences. In the pages of this book, we will delve into the necessary skills and mindset required to be effective stewards of our lives, ultimately leading to a fulfilling and purpose-driven existence.

WE ARE ALL CHOSEN

I chose to write this book because just as the characters I am writing about have personal stories of both tragedy and triumph, I too have a story. When I read the Bible, I feel a connection to the characters. Their lives make sense to me because I too am chosen and flawed. God has a plan for me, and my imperfections are not going to keep Him from using me. Consider the words of the apostle Paul.

> *"…but he said to me, 'My grace is sufficient for you,*
> *for my power is made perfect in weakness.'*
> *So I will boast all the more gladly of my weaknesses,*
> *so that the power of Christ may dwell in me."*
> —2 Corinthians 12:9

By choosing to boast of Christ's strength in my weakness, I find power, true power. When I can't move forward, when I get stuck in a dark place and can't find my way to the light, when I can't grow, when I can't forgive and receive healing, I must humble myself, confess my sin, and commit to obedience. Only then will I find my pain transformed into power. My failings are an opportunity for me to not only experience God's grace but to share it with others.

I'm writing this book for all of us who are struggling with the concept of how you can be both chosen and flawed at the same time. "Chosen" and "flawed" are not mutually exclusive ideas, despite what you may think. Both things can happen and coexist. We need to be reminded of this fact: to live a full and abundant life, we must accept that we are both chosen and flawed. This book is intended to encourage those who feel they are not worthy, that they are not good enough—those who feel that their failings have disqualified them from experiencing the blessings of walking with God.

Our brokenness does not have to define us or limit us. We should recognize and accept that the infinite God created us as imperfect, finite beings and that these "defects" are a part of our identity. He is our Creator and our Redeemer. We belong to Him, and He uses our imperfections for His glory. He did it with Adam and Eve. He did it with David. He did it with many other well-known Bible characters, whom you will read about in the following chapters. God chose them despite all of their flaws, because their flaws did not necessarily mean that they would not be used for God's plan.

You are chosen, adopted into His family, and equipped for good works that He has already planned and prepared for you (see Ephesians 2:10). Every generation always believes that their hardship is much worse than the previous generations. Based on current research and data, the times we are living in have truly created an emotional trauma unlike any we have seen in decades. The life we are experiencing post-COVID has altered the landscape of humanity in ways we've never imagined before. People are currently experiencing some of the highest levels of depression, anxiety, social isolation, and overall mental crisis at record numbers. Sometimes we need a reminder of a "normal" baseline we used to have and the possibility of re-establishing that baseline again by learning from our past. Sometimes that past has to be a place that existed thousands of years ago.

New Revised Standard Version (NRSV) Bible Citation:

For this book, I chose to use the NRSV version, updated 2021, of the Bible because of its modern use of the English language and ease of readability. I have done my best to quote various verses that I referenced in my analysis. But not all of the verses are written out, and it may be helpful to have a Bible close by in the version you prefer for further reading and to compare and contrast any verses quoted here.

Chapter 1

ADAM AND EVE

IN THE BEGINNING THERE WAS... EVE

> *"In the beginning when God created the heavens and the earth, the earth was a formless void and darkness covered the face of the deep, while a wind from God swept over the face of the waters."*
> —Genesis 1:1–2

In the beginning. Those are perhaps the most famous opening words in any book ever written. The origin of earth and all life on it, in fact the origin of all things, is laid out in the first book of the Old Testament. Humanity is born from the heart of God, man and woman fashioned from the elements, created as both an embodiment of and an expression of divine love.

The story of Adam and Eve has been shared over thousands of years with millions of people; their story has been told so many times, but most people tend to draw very similar lessons from them. How often have we heard the very important role that Adam played and how

God created him by breathing life into him, followed by the fact that Eve was created as a helpmate for Adam?

However, if we look more closely, there seem to be complications, even in divine love. Eve's story is one of great value; however, her perspective is rarely considered. We might ask: How did Eve get her name? What was her conversation with the serpent like?

By focusing on Eve—as a person, not as a symbol of the fall—we can explore and analyze the importance of communication and identity. These aspects are rarely considered when discussing this famous couple.

An important component of Adam's and Eve's identity formation was their environment. The Garden of Eden, wherever it was located, was a perfect place: pure and pristine—the environment, air, and water untainted by pollutants of any kind. There are very few such places left in the modern world, and you'd have to see them with your own eyes to believe they actually exist. Brain development was unimpeded and unaffected by any negativity, and one hundred percent of a human's mental capacity could be accessed. Adam's and Eve's brains knew what and how much to eat, and how to heal themselves from any injuries. Perhaps wounds healed themselves, naturally and quickly, or certain plants were used to assist the process.

Cell degeneration due to age and environmental factors is now an accepted scientific fact. In the twenty-first century, we are impressed by people reaching the age of one hundred. It's a huge achievement, and those who reach the milestone—or, better yet, go beyond it—are celebrated. People often ask them the secret to a long life. Is it eating right? Exercising regularly? Avoiding stress? What was the secret of long life in the beginning? In the beginning, there was no cell degeneration. People didn't fall apart as they aged. And death? There was no concept of death. How can you define something that has not been experienced?

Adam and Eve communicated with God directly since they were connected to Him through the highest forms of emotionality and understanding. Until God became flesh when Jesus was born, Adam and Eve were among only a few who were able to talk, stand, walk, and be in God's presence without being struck down. They perhaps communicated with God without the need for audible sounds or language, but were rather able to simply understand and be with God. They accepted this intimate relationship with God unconditionally without parameters or preconceived ideas of what God was supposed to be. Rather, to them, God was and always had been. The mind, body, and soul worked easily and efficiently together to enable them to not only conceptualize God but also fully appreciate Him. They were the perfect creations of a perfect God.

As the only people on Earth, Adam and Eve interacted only with God and the various creatures that God had created before He made the first man and first woman: his crowning work. Adam was constructed of the dirt as an adult male, into whose nostrils God breathed life. He entered a fully formed and functional world over which God gave him dominion. It was Adam who was given the task of naming the various beasts of the land, sea, and sky.

> *"Then the Lord God said, 'It is not good that the man should be alone; I will make him a helper as his partner.' So out of the ground the Lord God formed every animal of the field and every bird of the air, and brought them to the man to see what he would call them; and whatever the*

> *man called every living creature, that was its name.*
> *The man gave names to all cattle, and to the birds of the air,*
> *and to every animal of the field; but for the man there*
> *was not found a helper as his partner."*
> —Genesis 2:18–20

However, as the animals were of a lower order, not created in God's image as Adam was, they provided inadequate company for him. God recognized this and formed the woman Eve.

> *"So the Lord God caused a deep sleep to fall upon the man,*
> *and he slept; then, he took one of his ribs and closed up its place*
> *with flesh. And the rib that the Lord God had taken from the*
> *man he made into a woman and brought her to the man.*
> *Then the man said, 'This at last is bone of my bones and*
> *flesh of my flesh; this one shall be called Woman,*
> *for out of Man this one was taken.'"*
> —Genesis 2:21–23

We know virtually nothing of their behavior prior to the "fall." Verse 15 of Chapter 2 tells us that Adam worked maintaining the Garden. Eve presumably joined him in that labor after she was given to him as a "suitable helper." Verse 25 goes on to say that Adam and Eve were naked but felt no shame. Only God knows how they passed the time. With none of the sources of entertainment we take for granted these days, I guess you can use your imagination, as they probably did.

So, we have a perfect man, and a perfect woman, living together in a perfect place, where nothing troubles them and they want for nothing.

Adam and Eve's relationship was in the perfect environment, and all of their needs were met. They knew no shame, sadness, death, or sin while they lived in the Garden.

As the relationship progresses, they become more alike, mimicking certain behaviors and mannerisms over time. As Adam and Eve spent more time together, they got closer and closer, becoming like one person. This is also quite common in our own relationships. As individuals begin to spend more and more time together, we begin to grow a new identity. It's almost as if a third identity exists between couples the longer they coexist. The individual identity seems to fade away over years and years, and the third identity begins to take shape. This level of closeness or bonding allows individuals to have conversations of trust and often speak to one another without even saying any words because they seem to know what the other person's needs or wants may be as a result of knowing each other so well. However, keep in mind that this type of shift can happen in "toxic" relationships just as easily as in "healthy" ones.

So here we have Adam and Eve, living a perfect life of unity in the Garden of Eden. And then a variable enters into the picture: the serpent.

> *"Now the serpent was more crafty than any other wild animal that the Lord God had made. He said to the woman, 'Did God say, "You shall not eat from any tree in the garden"?'"*
> —GENESIS 3:1

God had planted two trees in the middle of the garden: the Tree of Life and the Tree of the Knowledge of Good and Evil. How often did

Eve pass by the trees and how often did she ponder what the fruit of the Tree of Knowledge of Good and Evil must have tasted like? How often did the serpent visit the garden? More importantly, how long had the serpent been watching Eve, waiting for the perfect opportunity to pounce on his prey when they could potentially be at their weakest? Similar to a predator in the wilderness, lying low in the grasslands, observing, and identifying the ideal "vulnerable" or "injured" prey to isolate and capture.

Before we jump into the very important dialogue between Eve and the serpent, we must ask the question: where was Adam during this conversation? It seems that the serpent chose to target Eve rather than Adam. Thus far in the first two chapters, Eve is simply referred to as the "woman" or "wife." No other identifiers. Adam, on the other hand, is given his name by God and is given the task of naming all of the animals and caring for the Garden. His wife is not given specific tasks; rather, she is charged with "helping."

And this time, Adam was nowhere to be found, which presented the golden opportunity to create a divide. The serpent must have realized that he could not weaken Adam since he must have had a closer relationship with God. The serpent sought the chance to go after Eve, since she may not have had the same sense of ownership over the Garden that Adam did. The "wife" or "woman" merely stayed behind, and the serpent used her as the proxy to create a divide between man and God.

Was the snake the devil, or did Satan simply possess it in order to carry out the evil plan to destroy paradise? The answer is neither here nor there. The important fact is that it was not God who spoke to Eve, suggesting she misheard or misunderstood God's instruction regarding the Tree of Knowledge of Good and Evil. Although the name of the tree implies that Adam and Eve would be able to obtain a higher form of thinking, it is also worth noting that God provided everything for Adam and Eve. All of their needs were met. They simply had to have faith in God and believe that God would continue to supply them exactly what they needed. However, God also allowed them—and us—to have free will. How often we are met with an opportunity when all of our needs are sufficiently met, but we constantly want more of something without ever realizing the "why" behind our desire.

Let's focus on the serpent's words. The serpent says, "Did God really say you must not eat of any tree in the garden?" Notice the lie, the serpent's misrepresentation of the instruction. The truth was that God said the opposite. He said they could eat from any tree except one. The beginning of the end of paradise—the origin of the fall—was a lie, and Satan is still destroying lives today with the same insidious tactic.

However, keep in mind that God had given Adam a clear instruction, which was fully repeated and most likely understood by Eve since she repeats the instruction in Genesis 3:2–3:

> "The woman said to the serpent, 'We may eat of the fruit of the trees in the garden; but God said, "You shall not eat of the fruit of the tree that is in the middle of the garden, nor shall you touch it, or you shall die."'"

Let's step back and consider the presence of a talking snake. There was no reason for her to be afraid as there was nothing to fear in her experience. There was no reason to doubt that what she was hearing and seeing was real. The biblical narrative suggests a very relaxed and casual conversation. The deception was a huge blindside move by the serpent on an unsuspecting and naturally trusting Eve. In Genesis 3:2–3, she corrects the serpent's lie, but even then there is no suggestion that she is in any trouble.

However, the conversation quickly takes a turn. In Genesis 3:4, having planted a seed of doubt in Eve's mind, the serpent boldly calls God a liar. *No Eve*, he says. *You will not die. You will simply be like God, knowing good and evil.* That seems to be all it took for Eve to cave in. Time spent in an unsafe conversation peppered with lies had weakened her trust in God to the point that suddenly the fruit on that tree, the proverbial forbidden fruit, looked attractive, tasty, and nutritious, and offered the added bonus of wisdom. Notice how knowledge of good and evil can make one "wise."

Naïve and innocent Eve was tricked by the serpent, who twisted the truth during a conversation that could have lasted some time. There might have been some back and forth on the topic, a healthy debate. The same words recorded in Genesis were potentially repeated any number of times. The serpent may have added a plaintive tone, begging Eve to be sensible and to do what was good for her. What could be wrong with that? The serpent might have flattered her, using sweet words to convince Eve to believe that he had her best interests at heart. It's easy to imagine Eve being worn down by the conversation and the seditious methods of the serpent.

If we were to ask who named Eve or how she got her name, most people might say that it was God who named her. In fact, it was Adam who finally gave her a name in Genesis 3:20: *"The man named his wife Eve, because she was the mother of all living."* Interestingly enough, Adam does not give Eve a name until after the fall of man. What would Eve's conversation with the serpent have been like if she would have had her own identity as Adam did? What would she have said to the serpent if Adam had encouraged or given Eve the same ownership or responsibility as he had? Would she have stood up to the serpent if she had been empowered by Adam? The exploration of identity is an important part of our culture, and if people are treated equally and fairly, stronger bonds can exist. Even in our own lives, after a prolonged period in a relationship, one identity may consume another and an imbalance begin to take shape. Then people will often say to themselves, *What happened to me? Who have I become? I don't even know who I am anymore.* It's important to coexist in a relationship without losing sight of your own identity or self.

While Eve was hard work for Satan, Adam appears to have surrendered very meekly. The first forty words of Genesis 3:6 describe Eve's act of disobedience; the last fifteen words say this: "*…and she also gave some to her husband, who was with her, and he ate.*" Just like that. He ate the fruit, but he didn't say anything. Why? Why didn't he stop her? Not only did he not stop her, but he joined in after a simple invitation. She didn't even say anything. She simply handed the forbidden fruit to Adam, and he ate it.

Unfortunately, even though Adam knew God had instructed him not to eat the fruit, he still disregarded his Father's commandment. We see the perfect example of the third identity existing between couples as Adam ate the fruit without further inquiring where or how Eve had acquired it. He followed his wife into poor decision-making rather than stopping and asking a few simple questions like, "Where did you get this fruit?" or "Who gave it to you?" Rather, he blindly just took and ate of it. A momentary pause could have given Adam a moment of clarity. Although this may seem contrary to being in a secure and stable relationship, asking clear and information-seeking questions can be part of having healthy communication skills. Asking questions with the proper tone, pitch, pace, and patience will lead to effective communication and create a healthier environment. Blind trust and faith in each other can lead to conflict, and striving to create healthier communication skills can lead to a better understanding of one another.

It is also worth noting that when Eve ate the fruit, her eyes were not opened. Only when Adam ate the fruit were both of their eyes opened.

> *"Then the eyes of both were opened, and they knew that they were naked; and they sewed fig leaves together and made loincloths for themselves."*
> —Genesis 3:7

Would Eve have faced death all by herself if Adam had refused the forbidden fruit? God had given the commandment not to eat to Adam, not Eve. So, all these years, we've been blaming Eve for the fall of man, when in reality Adam was the responsible party. Could the "fall" of man have been avoided if Adam had done his due diligence of practicing some basic communication skills? What would the outcome have been had Adam given Eve her name—her identity—when they first met rather than waiting for them to be kicked out of the garden?

Neither Adam nor Eve felt any shame in their nakedness until their "eyes were opened." The idea of body shaming or being ashamed of our physical beauty has clearly created an unhealthy mental state for individuals of all ages. Here is the truth: God sees us as perfect, and we diminish our physical self because of the unattainable standards falsely set by society, especially social media. These unattainable standards can often create internal and external struggles.

One final point to consider in this unfortunate story of paradise lost is when God called out to Adam and Eve in the garden—saying *"Where are you?"* (Genesis 3:9)—He already knew the answer. We must ask what God's response would have been if Adam and Eve had merely apologized and taken responsibility for eating the forbidden fruit. Adam was quick to blame Eve, who, in turn, was quick to blame the serpent. At no point was there an apology, an expression of remorse, or an acceptance of responsibility. They were too busy projecting blame and trying to come up with a story. We'll never know how differently things might have turned out if Adam and Eve had simply confessed and repented of their sin.

One of the key takeaways from Adam and Eve's story is the value of identity and effective communication. We diminish people, and yet we choose to live a false reality that everyone is created equal. Even biblically we are to be equal, but then countless women are suppressed and can only do something when the man provides guidance. If Eve had a sense of ownership, identity, and purpose, would she have been manipulated by the serpent? If Adam had made her part of the solution rather than part of the problem, would she have been easily persuaded? Eve only had as much ownership of the garden as Adam allowed or "bestowed" upon her.

Additionally, in terms of effective communication, people stop posing questions even when additional information is desperately needed to make a rational decision. This inaction is often due to individuals believing that posing additional questions may cause some type of argument or conflict. But by asking clarifying questions and having direct communication, we may learn that we can get along much more effectively with one another rather than fearing the worst outcome. As you read through this book, you will see that God is very clear in communicating with His children. However, mankind has a way of altering the information in our brains before we either pass it on or act upon what was instructed. Being steadfast in practicing effective communication can lead to a faithful relationship with God.

The consequence of the original sin, committed first by Eve and then by Adam, is catastrophic. Paradise was lost and sold cheaply, and the rest of the Word of God is all about God's mission to restore paradise and to reconcile all people to Himself. As we see in the following chapters, being "chosen" and "flawed" has its benefits and its consequences since now the stage is set because of the choices Adam and Eve made in the Garden. Certainty remains that life at times will be difficult, but we often make it even more complicated when we allow our flaws to overtake the purpose of our chosen journey.

It is in these moments of struggle and imperfection that we must remember the ultimate goal of restoration and reconciliation. Despite our flaws and the consequences of the original sin, God's love and grace are always present, guiding us back toward paradise. It is through acknowledging our mistakes, seeking forgiveness, and striving to live according to God's will that we can begin to unravel the complexities we have created in our lives. As we navigate the challenges of being both chosen and flawed, let us hold onto the hope of redemption and the promise of a renewed paradise where we are fully reconciled to God.

Chapter 2

CAIN AND ABEL

NOT-SO-BROTHERLY LOVE

The story of Cain and Abel is covered in its entirety in less than sixteen verses in the Bible. One could argue that an analysis would be difficult to conduct with such little information. I would argue that oftentimes there is assessment data when little or nothing is said. We will attempt to understand the personalities of Cain and Abel as they relate to their jobs. We will also begin to understand their relationship with each other as well as with their parents, Adam and Eve. Through this analysis, we learn that the values of self-reflection and confirmation bias play a dramatic role in Cain's life.

As part of the new reality facing Adam and Eve after God banished them from the Garden of Eden, God told Eve that her joy in childbearing would be saddened by the pain of it. It is variously described in different translations of Genesis 3:16 as a multiplication of pain in childbirth (The Message), and much trouble and great pain in childbirth (NRSV). Irrespective of the wording, childbirth and indeed being pregnant, while still joyous, are full of intense pain, as many women have learned firsthand throughout the centuries. Adam's role post-paradise would also involve pain: the pain of hard labor (Genesis 3:17–19). Forced to leave that perfect place and prevented from re-entering it, Adam and Eve began a new life together. They were still blessed. God had not cursed them, but He did show them there were consequences for disobedience.

Adam became a farmer in earnest, involving himself with agriculture and animal husbandry, and Eve would have assisted with those tasks.

> *"Now [Adam] knew his wife Eve, and she conceived and bore Cain, saying, 'I have produced a man with the help of the Lord.'"*
> —GENESIS 4:1

One can assume that Adam and Eve made love in the Garden of Eden, but it appears Eve didn't become pregnant until after their exile from Eden. After Cain, she gave birth to Abel (Genesis 4:2). We aren't told what the age gap was, but it is safe to say around a year. Cain and Abel were most likely close in age.

We don't know anything else about these boys except that Cain became a tiller of the land, a farmer, and Abel a caretaker of the animals—two equally valid and essential occupations which were either chosen by Cain and Abel themselves or assigned by their father. Perhaps the two occupations reflected the boys' interests in addition to their personalities. There may have been other things that were easier for Abel as the "baby" of the family. Much is expected of eldest children, whereas the baby of the family is often given more leeway in many families. Adam may have favored one of his sons over the other. Eve might have had a similar preference. We don't know. The Bible doesn't tell us anything about the boys, what they did apart from work, or how they got along with each other and their parents.

Firstborn son Cain, toiling hard on the land as a farmer, had animosity toward Abel for being the younger sibling, and possibly resented Abel for having the easier job. Looking after animals was probably an easier job or perceived as more desirable than growing crops. Cain's days were spent waiting for crops to grow, a slow and arduous process that required backbreaking work in the fields under the scorching sun or bitter cold. Constantly tilling, planting, watering, and harvesting, he returned to the fields day after day, yearning to see progress. The isolation of farm life may have driven Cain to introspection, his mind consumed with negative thoughts and endless rumination.

Abel, as a caretaker of the animals, had company. Some of his work would have been done alone as well—let's not forget there were only four people in the world at that time—but at least he had the company of the animals he looked after. He could talk to them, and they would listen. Science has proven the benefits of spending time with animals, which arise from the release of pleasurable and relaxing hormones such as dopamine, oxytocin, and serotonin. Companion animals improve people's well-being. At the least, Abel had that, even if he did occasionally long for more human company. We can only speculate about what level of communion he and the others in his family had with God.

In short, the relationship between Cain and Abel was one of sibling rivalry. I have often found that the quality of my relationship with my brothers ebbs and flows. Oftentimes siblings will hold grudges for years even though they can't remember what upset them and caused the rift in the first place. If your family is not affected by such division, thank God, but for sure you know at least one family that has suffered or is suffering through family estrangement and bitterness. We are not given much time on this earth, and if we continue to live our lives in anger and frustration with our brothers and sisters, it may be too late when we realize what a waste of time it was.

This first family still prayed and offered sacrifices as a form of worship, although the Bible does not tell us how these practices came about. In the Garden, Adam and Eve had direct communication with their Creator, but things were different now. Sin had entered the world, and the most serious consequence and immediate impact was probably a loss of communion with God. The practice of bringing gifts—making offerings to God—seems to have arisen organically. There is no suggestion in the scripture that the sacrifices or offerings were for atonement, as most of the sacrifices were later to become as part of the Mosaic Law. The gifts brought to God by Cain and Abel were freewill offerings, most likely of gratitude but perhaps also of petition, that God would continue to bless the work of their hands.

> *"In the course of time Cain brought to the Lord*
> *an offering of the fruit of the ground, and Abel for his part*
> *brought of the firstlings of his flock, their fat portions.*
> *And the Lord had regard for Abel and his offering,*
> *but for Cain and his offering he had no regard.*
> *So Cain was very angry, and his countenance fell."*
> —Genesis 4:3–5

On the surface this seems unfair and is maybe the first instance of discrimination. Why was God pleased with Abel's offering but displeased with Cain's? Verse 4 says Abel gave the best parts of the firstborn of his animals. Was it the offering itself that God found acceptable or Abel's attitude? Was it that God, who always judges rightly, knew Abel gave with a good heart, as an expression of gratitude and worship, not expecting anything in return? Surely God knew that about Abel, even before he presented this world-changing offering.

Cain gave too, but significantly, there is no mention of "first" or "best" to describe his offering, and just as God knew Abel, he also knew Cain. Cain's gift was given begrudgingly. He didn't give the best of his crop, and he gave with a downward countenance (he wasn't happy about giving what he felt was his). We are told that was how Cain reacted to his offering being rejected, but as with Abel, God knew him before that. God knew his heart, his motive, and his attitude, and He called Cain out, asking him directly.

> *"The Lord said to Cain, 'Why are you angry, and why has your countenance fallen? If you do well, will you not be accepted? And if you do not do well, sin is lurking at the door; its desire is for you, but you must master it.'"*
> —Genesis 4:6–7

Interestingly, Cain's answer is not recorded. Perhaps the question was rhetorical. Perhaps Cain chose to remain silent and sullen. Maybe he believed he didn't have to give as much as Abel because his perception was that he worked harder than his brother. Oftentimes, even in our own lives, we feel that we work harder than others. *Where is my reward? Where is my recognition? Why is Abel getting all the kudos?* Can you feel the resentment building, boiling within Cain? Cain thought he would never be good enough, that he would never measure up. Not only did his parents favor Abel over him, but even God preferred the younger son of Adam. What could he do about that? Can you imagine how he felt? If we are being honest, I am sure we can. You have probably felt the same way yourself at some time in your life, or even now as you read these words.

Cain didn't answer God's question, so God continued telling him what He thought of the situation. It was another rejection. Another reason for Cain to feel he would never be good enough. God noted that Cain was upset and, despite His original question, He knew why. God told Cain not to worry. Just give with a good heart and give faithfully. His words were intended to be an encouragement to Cain, but Cain probably received them as a chilling warning. The words were, "...*And if you do not do well, sin is lurking at the door; its desire is for you, but you must master it.*" With prophetic words, God told Cain that sin was lurking at his door. Of course, God knew that Cain was going to murder his brother, Abel. He spoke to Cain as He did to let him know that he was in danger. Cain's emotions and feelings of not being able to control his physical response were only a further acknowledgment of his inability to maintain self-control. Up to this point, Cain potentially felt inadequate or under-appreciated due to his continued negative talk from his perceived incessant, backbreaking hard labor.

This moment in Cain's life could also be viewed as confirmation bias, a psychological term for the human tendency to only seek out information that supports one position or idea. It essentially means an individual already has predisposed ideas about a potential outcome and the results only confirm those predisposed ideas. Unfortunately, human nature often puts us on a path where individuals may perform certain acts either consciously or subconsciously to obtain a known outcome... confirmation bias. They may even commit self-sabotaging behaviors to adopt a victim mentality in the hopes of garnering some level of sympathy from friends, family members, or even complete strangers if the situation dictates. In Cain's case, his belief that his efforts were not being valued or recognized may have fueled his confirmation bias. This could have pushed him to seek validation in ways that inadvertently caused his own downfall. Instead of confronting his feelings of inadequacy directly, he may have unconsciously taken actions that led to the tragic event between him and his brother Abel.

One day, Cain and Abel were in the field talking when Cain struck and killed his little brother. It was no accident, no crime of passion. Cain didn't suddenly lose it in the field that day. It was a premeditated murder. Genesis 4:8 tells us that Cain invited his brother into the field. Abel might have wondered why, but he went anyway, trusting his brother. Perhaps Abel was pleased with the opportunity to spend time with Cain to mend some fences between them; maybe he was feeling hopeful as he went to meet his brother.

God approached Cain immediately, or soon after the murder, and asked Cain where his brother was. Try to visualize Cain working in the field on his hands and knees when God walks up on him and poses the question. I doubt that Cain ever even looked up at God. Perhaps he was scared, annoyed, or even so narcissistic as to have completely "forgotten" he had just murdered his brother.

> "Then the Lord said to Cain, 'Where is your brother Abel?'"
> —GENESIS 4:9

Why would God ask a question to which He knew the answer? Before Abel's murder, there were four people on the entire earth, and now there were only three. Imagine God's pain speaking to Cain. One of his children had taken the life of another. Cain never showed remorse and was completely lacking in empathy because he answered God with a question. A question that has now become a proverb in our language—what someone says when they don't want to take responsibility for a person. A cop-out adage.

> *"He said, 'I do not know; am I my brother's keeper?'"*
> —Genesis 4:9

This is an interesting response from Cain. Most would ask or wonder if Cain's response was out of fear or attempting to hide his crime. I would argue, neither. I don't believe he was afraid because everyone is born with only two innate fears—the fear of falling and loud sounds. Everything else is learned. If Cain was afraid, his fear response would have been fight or flight. His brain would have released adrenaline, which would have caused increased blood to his major organs and extremities along with quicker breathing. One would expect, through natural human response tendencies, that Cain would have reacted with at least some level of concern after taking his brother's life. However, Cain had not learned fear in the moments after killing Abel, which might sound odd, but remember, the world was new and this was the first death. Who is to say that he did not feel some sense of peace of not having to deal with Abel anymore? Thus the lack of remorse or empathy.

The question also shows God's mercy and grace. When God asked Cain about Abel, Cain could have confessed and asked for forgiveness, just as his parents could have done in the Garden when they ate the forbidden fruit and God confronted them. God would have forgiven them, and he would have forgiven Cain. There would have been consequences for his actions but possibly not as great as the punishment he eventually received. Only God knows what was in Cain's heart as He pronounced His judgment on the elder son of the first man and woman.

> *"And now you are cursed from the ground,*
> *which has opened its mouth to receive your brother's*
> *blood from your hand. When you till the ground,*
> *it will no longer yield to you its strength; you will*
> *be a fugitive and a wanderer on the earth."*
> —Genesis 4:11–12

We may make mistakes in our lives, and it can often seem easier to try and hide them rather than confess and tell the truth. We may be able to deceive others, but God already knows the answers to the questions He may ask us. Are we going to try to hide from the truth and suffer the full consequences of our actions? Or will we confess our sins, receive God's forgiveness, and with grace accept the consequences and move on?

Cain's response, in context, is predictable. He was only worried about his well-being. He didn't try to justify or even explain himself, nor apologize. Interestingly, the curse was not upon Cain himself, but upon the ground. If he thought it was hard growing crops before, he was in for a rude awakening. God effectively turned him into a nomad, a wanderer. Knowing the seriousness of this punishment, Cain still did not show any empathy, and only cared about himself.

> *"Cain said to the Lord, 'My punishment is greater than I can bear! Today you have driven me away from the soil, and I shall be hidden from your face; I shall be a fugitive and a wanderer on the earth, and anyone who meets me may kill me.'"*
> —Genesis 4:13–14

God placed a mark upon Cain that effectively protected him from physical harm. Remarkable grace, isn't it? Anyone who brought harm to Cain would thereafter be subject to sevenfold revenge. The mark could have been placed upon his skin, or it could have been a horn protruding from his back, but in any case, the warning is clear and everyone would know it. Cain is left to wander through the wild, and later marries one of his sisters and has children. Cain establishes cities for his children, and his children have children, whose lineage is traced down through the generations (Genesis 4:17–22). The population of God's new world grows and the message about the mark of Cain is shared to all.

Cain and Abel's story is often taught from a perspective of Cain's egregious behaviors and his actions. However, his story is also a reminder of how powerful confirmation bias can be in shaping our thoughts, emotions, and behaviors, often without us even realizing it. Additionally, Cain's story serves as a cautionary tale about the importance of self-awareness and challenging our own biases in order to avoid self-destructive patterns of behavior. While the consequences of his unwillingness or inability to confess his sins and repent of them were serious and lasting, and his flaws were apparent, Cain was still chosen to further God's plan for humanity. He lived, raised a large family, and established a city. Here, we see God's grace in action once more.

Chapter 3

NOAH

BEING A HERO CAN BE TRAUMATIC

God may have extended His grace to Cain and his descendants, but things were not all right in the world. Chapter 6 of Genesis tells us that the wickedness of mankind was increasing, and that God was grieved by His children wandering further and further away from Him.

> "The Lord saw that the wickedness of humankind was great in the earth, and that every inclination of the thoughts of their hearts was only evil continually."
> —Genesis 6:5

This brings us to the story of Noah, perhaps one of the most well-known of the Old Testament. However, we often learn this story of Noah's accomplishment without considering the human factor. Noah was chosen by God to save mankind from complete annihilation and to continue the lineage that was needed in order for Jesus to enter the world. The first six hundred years of Noah's life fulfilled him and brought him purpose. He is seen as a man who carried out God's instructions perfectly, without question. Unfortunately, as it has been stated in the Bible numerous times, our life of faith will certainly not be easy and our belief in the Almighty will be tested. There will be stages of pain and suffering, as there were for Noah.

When Noah's father, Lamech, named him, he said, *"Out of the ground that the Lord has cursed this one shall bring us relief from our work and from the toil of our hands"* (Genesis 5:29). Talk about laying some heavy expectations on a child. We know nothing of the extent to which Noah fulfilled his father's wishes or whether Lamech's words were prophetic in any sense, but we do know that Noah knew what his name meant and would likely have labored under the expectation of his father and perhaps others in the extended family—that he was to be some kind of savior.

Irrespective of what Lamech thought, or what Noah did, the former died before seeing anything significant happen other than the birth of three grandsons: Shem, Ham, and Japheth.

By this stage most of God's beloved creatures had run off the rails, and God was displeased. Noah, on the other hand, found favor with God (Genesis 6:8–9). Noah was a righteous man who was blameless in his generation. Was Noah aware of how highly God regarded him? Not likely. One rarely finds pride and righteousness (meaning rightness with God) present in the same person.

Had he lived, Lamech would have been super proud to see Noah's success. In the midst of a corrupt world, God chooses Noah to be a savior. In fact, God speaks to Noah, revealing His plan to destroy "all flesh" on the earth—except for Noah and his family (Genesis 6:13–18). Imagine how Noah must have felt to hear from God that the world would be destroyed by flood but Noah himself and his family would be saved. How would you respond to such news?

God further showed Noah how he was to be saved and what he had to do: he was to build an ark, or large boat, with specific dimensions, and gather together two of each kind of animal and bird, as well as provisions for all aboard. In giving His righteous servant a set of very detailed instructions, God showed Noah He was serious. Even if Noah doubted, he still obeyed. He built the ark according to the specifications God gave him. Most likely Noah was able to get various people to help him build the ark, including his family. The final product was approximately 510 feet long, 85 feet wide, and about 51 feet tall, and likely took many years to complete. It was a truly monumental construction task. After the ark was constructed, the animals were brought on board.

God not only gave Noah instructions for building the ark and directions concerning who and what should be on it, He also made a covenant with Noah, promising him that he would survive the coming catastrophe. When the order was given to fill the ark with two of every kind of animal, including one pair of each unclean animal and seven pairs of each clean animal (Genesis 7:2–3), the countdown to the end of the world was on. Noah was told that forty days and forty nights of rain would begin in seven days' time.

Imagine the ridicule Noah would have received from others as he devoted perhaps decades of his life to building that ark. Although there is no biblical record of his words, we can assume he simply told people what God had said to him. As John the Baptist was a *"voice crying in the wilderness"* (Mark 1:3), so perhaps Noah was a lone voice speaking out against the sinful world. Or maybe he worked in silence. He must have questioned the value of his work at times. There would have been setbacks, disappointments, and doubts. Many people would have thought he was mad, written him off as an eccentric fool. It was business as usual for the people of that time, as Jesus said in Matthew 24:38: *"For as in those days before the flood they were eating and drinking, marrying and giving in marriage, until the day Noah entered the ark."*

Noah endured the mockery, every unkind word, every snide remark, as he obediently continued his work. When the ark was complete and the animals had been loaded, Noah and his family—his wife and his three sons and their wives—joined them, and God shut the door (Genesis 7:16). If Noah needed any more encouragement besides having heard the voice of God on several occasions, this final act of God closing the door of the ark to seal them inside must have been a moment of intense emotion. Noah may have had to calm his family, to reassure them that God would protect them. He must also have calmed the animals, soothing and settling them as they waited for the rain. Outside the ark, which sat on the dry ground and was as useful as a car without wheels, the taunting continued for seven days, but Noah did not waver. It was too late anyway. Their fate was sealed. Noah was a man with the weight of the world on his shoulders as he waited patiently for the rain God had promised. A supernatural peace filled not only his heart but the whole ark.

The deluge began in the six hundredth year of Noah's life. The people celebrated the coming of the rain, continuing to heap scorn on Noah, but as the water rose, they began begging and pleading with Noah to save them. Noah remained steadfast, and in truth, there was nothing he could do because God had shut the door, and only He could open it. As the ground was pummeled mercilessly by heavy rain, it began to flood, and Noah shifted into survival mode. It was really happening. Adrenaline kicked in. Pretty soon he began to hear people dying all around him. People crying and taking their last breath: men, women, and children crying and screaming. His closest neighbors, friends, and extended family members, whom he had lived with for 600 years, drowning in the waters, clawing and clamoring to climb aboard the ark and save themselves, but all to no avail.

He probably saw numerous faces he recognized disappear into the waters. Probably made eye contact with some of those folks, possibly helped or tried to help some of them. Maybe as many as he could. Remember, Noah was still a kind, loving, friendly, family-loving man, a righteous and merciful man. He knew God was right and just, but he still felt the pain of the Creator's judgment on his neighbors.

When there was enough water, the ark was lifted from the ground and began to drift. It had no means of propulsion or steering. The ark and all the living creatures locked inside it were at the whim of the mighty and tempestuous waters that soon covered the whole earth.

Noah and his sons worked aboard the ark, cleaning and feeding the animals. He kept himself busy trying to survive during that time and did not necessarily process all of his sad thoughts. Distracted with what needed to be done, he did not have time to consider his loss or to grieve.

Finally, after a 150-day flood event, the likes of which the world had never seen nor has seen since that time, the ark came to a rest on a mountain. After another couple of months, the land was dry and God released the occupants of the ark, telling Noah and his family to go forth and multiply. The first thing Noah did when he got out of the ark was to build an altar and offer a clean animal sacrifice to God to say thank you.

Noah became a farmer and a family man. He planted a vineyard and was the first winemaker in the Bible. He could have done anything, grown anything, but he decided to plant grapes and learn how to make wine. He evidently took a strong liking to wine. Verse 21 of Chapter 9 in Genesis tells us that Noah got drunk. Not tipsy. Not slightly inebriated. But fall-down drunk, and at least once, he passed out from drinking too much. On this particular occasion, we are told that he was found naked in his tent by his son Ham, who was embarrassed by his father's behavior.

> *"He drank some of the wine and became drunk, and he lay uncovered in his tent. And Ham, the father of Canaan, saw the nakedness of his father, and told his two brothers outside. Then Shem and Japheth took a garment, laid it on both their shoulders, and walked backward and covered the nakedness of their father; their faces were turned away, and they did not see their father's nakedness."*
> —Genesis 9:21–23

Noah was angry when he found out what happened, and rather than accepting blame for his drunken state and his way of living, he cursed his son Ham and kicked him out of the land.

Why would Noah act this way? It is possible, because he was traumatized, that he recalled all those voices he heard and the pain he felt from all of the people dying. He in some way felt that he was to blame because he didn't save anyone except for his immediate family. He was depressed, developed anxiety, and perhaps even contemplated suicide. How could a person not feel the effects of such an event and blame himself for every human being on earth dying while he did nothing to save any of them? This moment in time captures a man going through post-traumatic stress disorder (PTSD) or perhaps survivor's guilt. One does not have to go to war or endure a military conflict when they are suffering from PTSD. Any perceived traumatic event could create an emotional imprint, potentially leading to PTSD. Even after following God's plan perfectly, Noah stumbled and succumbed to the negative outflowing of his trauma. He turned to alcohol to help him deal with the pain and suffering caused by the flood.

Noah's first six hundred years are discussed in three chapters. His last 350 years are summed up in just two verses.

> "After the flood Noah lived three hundred fifty years.
> All the days of Noah were nine hundred fifty years; and he died."
> —Genesis 9:28–29

Noah spent his last 350 years in a drunken state, traumatized and unable to deal with what happened on the ark. He struggled with alcoholism, depression, anxiety, and PTSD. What a sad way for a great man to end his life, and yet, I am sure he was accepted into the loving arms of his merciful Father, the God who called on him and whom he obeyed at great personal cost.

Noah too was flawed, and God knew what would become of him after the ark. However, that did not prevent God from choosing him. If Noah would have allowed God to heal him, then who knows? Maybe he would have lived out his last 350 years with some level of contentment, happiness, and joy. Instead, he wallowed in sadness, fear, and depression. Look around! Almost everyone is certainly dealing with some level of sadness, fear, anxiety, and depression. It might be you or someone close to you. At the heart of these emotions is a feeling of hopelessness, but we must never forget that if God chose Noah to carry out His will, regardless of his flaws, then God can also help us deal with all of those emotions felt by Noah so that we can start the path to recovery, healing, and the happiness we all seek.

Chapter 4

JOB

SUFFERING IN LOUD SILENCE

The Book of Job is controversial because Job's whole world is turned upside down for no apparent or acceptable reason, at least to the reader. He does nothing wrong to deserve such terrible misfortunes. Job's life was completely torn apart for a test of faith, which often leaves readers conflicted by the content, and questioning God's motives. Even other biblical prophets may not have known what to do with his story; Job is only referenced one other time in the Bible, when James uses him as a model of patience in suffering (James 5:11). People often ask why God would allow an innocent man to go through such a series of devastating losses. Job did nothing to merit the level of pain and suffering that he endured. We may feel the same way about events in our own lives or in the lives of others. It's an age-old question that has frequently been used to deny the existence of a loving God, because how could a loving God allow suffering, especially to the extreme that Job endured?

Job's story is complicated, and the following is to be taken only as an analysis—a discussion of the facts presented in the Bible. Job was accused of being a sinner, the assumption being that his suffering was punishment for those sins. But in the end Job, even though he said some unfortunate things about God, was not chastised for questioning God, and the end result of his suffering was great reward. Yet we can learn more from this story than that our suffering might eventually be rewarded.

People often read the Bible and take it at face value, adopting the simple view that the message is straightforward. However, it often isn't. It's multi-layered. When we begin to uncover the Word and the messages within the text, we begin to see a picture developing. When I'm trying to assess people in my role as an investigator, I must drop all of my bias and predisposed ideas about an individual and assess them on face value, examining and testing what I see, what they say, and how they say it. I must keep an open mind and weigh the information presented to me objectively. I encourage you to challenge yourself to do likewise, always remembering that only God knows everything.

God allows things to happen in our lives for a reason. He doesn't do anything without a reason. He doesn't act randomly or thoughtlessly. During a specific crisis, nothing seems to make sense, but when we look back after quite some time has passed, we may be able to discern some purpose for our suffering. As a result of a terrible circumstance occurring in our lives, we may learn something or even gain something. We must always remember "*... that in everything God works for good with those who love him, who are called according to his purpose*" (Romans 8:28, RSV).

Is it possible Job is simply an allegory told to show God's love, mercy, and compassion? What if the author was projecting himself as Job, a character he invented, trying to show that no matter what, God is ultimately in control? Even if Satan has you in his clutches and is refusing to let go, the Almighty is sovereign. Perhaps this tragic story should be read as a parable, a story of faithfulness and dedication.

With its themes of resilience, grief, sadness, strength in God, and family and friends, what can we learn from this book, from the series of tragedies that struck Job and how he responded? And what, if anything, did Job learn? How can we grieve loss and experience an unwelcome flood of negative emotions brought on by a tragedy in our lives, yet still encounter God's love? How can we be sure that He does really love us despite our circumstances and irrespective of how we feel about them? To discuss who Job is and why his story matters so much, we must begin to unpack a story that appears simple yet is very layered.

As the story begins in Job 1:1, we are introduced to a man named Job who lived in the land of Uz. Although the Bible doesn't say specifically where Uz was, it was east of Midian, probably in the land that became known as Edom (modern-day Syria and Jordan). This is an old story, with no reference to Mosaic Law or even the Children of Israel, suggesting that Job lived before Jacob. Job's lineage is not included, which is strange given the Bible's emphasis on genealogy.

Job was described as a man *"blameless and upright, one who feared God and turned away from evil"* (Job 1:1). He had seven sons and three daughters, and an impressive level of wealth. He was most likely one of the wealthiest men of his time. Job's life seemed to be a harmonious one, and his children seemed to get along with one another as described in verse 4, since all the siblings often ate together. There is no mention of specific acts of worship, though Job does make sacrifices on behalf of his children.

So, if we step back and take a look at Job and his life, what we have is a man who is doing exactly what is asked of him in order to serve God. He fears, loves, and worships God. He is one of the few men in the Bible referred to as being "perfect." Even though it does not say that Job is without sin, in this context "perfect" would most likely mean that Job was obedient in every way to God. In other words, he served God perfectly.

In the next part of this story, the scene changes. Verses 6 through 12 of the first chapter present the strange and unique scenario of God and Satan talking to one another. Presumably many such conversations took place, although perhaps their chats were less frequent and less congenial after Lucifer's rebellion, which resulted in him and a third of the angels being kicked out of Heaven. Whether or not the conversation recorded in Job actually happened or is merely an allegory is beside the point. It is possible the author wrote verses 6 through 12 to explain why Job's life suddenly went to ruin. It is also possible the Spirit of God, who inspired all scripture, gave the author a revelation; perhaps he saw it in a dream, then wrote it down.

In either case, the question remains: If God protected people from suffering, of course they would be grateful and obedient, but what if things didn't go well? Surely, thought Satan, if God were to remove that protection, they would abandon Him.

> *"But stretch out your hand now, and touch all that he has, and he will curse you to your face."*
>
> —JOB 1:11

Satan was suggesting that God's people were fair-weather followers, and he aimed to prove his point with Job, who lived such a blessed life that it was impossible for him to be anything other than the faithful servant he was. God granted Satan permission to attack Job but warned him he was not allowed to stretch out his hand against Job, only against what Job had (Job 1:12). That's an important distinction. In effect, God told Satan to keep his hands off Job.

The test began with the murder of Job's servants, the theft and destruction of his property, and the deaths of his children. With all the hardships that Job faced, he still kept his faith in God, although he experienced anguish, grievance, discouragement, and every other emotion he could possibly feel as a natural response to his circumstances. Yet he never gave up. Job never gave up being faithful.

> *"In all this Job did not sin or charge*
> *God with wrongdoing."*
> —JOB 1:22

Consider what Job went through for the sake of proving Satan wrong. Why did God feel the need to do that? Satan is always wrong because he is full of sin. What was the point of this horrific trial? To be honest, the question makes me feel uncomfortable. It makes me question God, which I don't like to do, but I remind myself that God is more than big enough to handle my doubts and questions.

Chapter 2 of the book was round 2. Satan returned to the throne room of God, having achieved nothing but being unwilling to admit he was wrong. Satan argued for a change to the rules of engagement, whereby he no doubt felt confident he would finally prove his point.

> *"But stretch out your hand now and touch his bone and his flesh, and he will curse you to your face."*
>
> —JOB 2:5

Again God agreed, but He imposed a condition on the arrangement, saying that Satan was not allowed to kill Job. Any form of torture was presumably permissible. Again, this is awkward for me as it should be for all of us. It is difficult to understand why God would allow such horrific things to happen to individuals just to see if they would remain faithful. The protection of Job's life is a reminder to us that God is the only one who can give life and the only one who can take it away.

After Satan inflicted Job with sores all over his body (2:7), his wife told him to curse God and die (2:9), but in verse 10 it is noted that *"in all this Job did not sin with his lips."*

Job's four friends then came along to allegedly comfort him. This section of the Book of Job is not often discussed, but it brings to light a key lesson: how we respond to adversity—both our own and that of others.

Chapters 3 to 37 describe in detail the long conversation between the four men and Job about Job's situation. Each friend visits Job during his time of suffering and offers his perspective, attempting to make sense of Job's hardships. These friends play significant roles in the narrative, representing different aspects of human nature, different beliefs, and different responses to adversity. This conversation features bold, even absurd claims—given the circumstances—of God's goodness and majesty. There are also curses against and lies about the Creator. At times, Job was encouraged to continue his faithful praise, while at other times he was advised to kill himself and be done with it all. The conversation contains a mix of truth and lies, often straying into hyperbole and parody until finally God joins the discussion. Throughout this conversation, we see hints of Job's great grief at his circumstances.

In the tale of Job, he finds himself weary not only in body but also in spirit. Despite understanding that he cannot contend with the power of God, Job's despondency reaches its lowest ebb. There are moments when being on our knees is insufficient; instead, prostrating ourselves on the ground, to the very depths, both physically and metaphorically, is necessary in order to reach God. Job's primary flaw lies in his lack of faith in the magnificence and mercy of God. He is ensnared in a cycle of negative self-doubt, where his anguish and gloom become his prevailing reality. Overcoming such a profound loss makes it increasingly challenging to find a path toward positivity.

The uncertainty of when his suffering will cease compounds Job's fear, leaving him adrift in a sea of despair. As he grapples with the unknown duration of his tribulations, Job's endurance is tested to its limits. He questions why he must endure such anguish and hardship, wondering if there will ever be a reprieve from his suffering. In those dark moments, Job's faith wavers, and he struggles to see the light at the end of the tunnel.

Yet, even in the depths of his despair, Job clings to a glimmer of hope. He knows that he must persevere, trusting that God has a plan for him, even if he cannot see it in the midst of his turmoil. Job's journey is a testament to the resilience of the human spirit, showing that even in the face of overwhelming adversity, faith can be a guiding light toward redemption and renewal.

Eliphaz the Temanite is the first friend to speak to Job and takes a traditional and conservative approach to the situation. He believes in the concept of divine retribution, suggesting that Job's suffering must be a result of his sins. Eliphaz represents the voice of conventional wisdom and religious orthodoxy, emphasizing the importance of repentance and submission to God's will.

Bildad the Shuhite follows Eliphaz in offering his perspective to Job. He reflects a more legalistic and rigid stance, insisting that suffering is a direct consequence of sin. Bildad represents the voice of judgment and moral absolutism, emphasizing the need for Job to acknowledge his guilt and seek forgiveness.

Zophar the Naamathite is the third friend to address Job and continues the theme of attributing suffering to sin. He portrays a harsh and unforgiving attitude, urging Job to confess his wrongdoings and accept his punishment. Zophar represents the voice of cruel judgment and a rigid adherence to moral principles, lacking compassion and understanding.

Elihu, the son of Barachel the Buzite, appears later in the narrative and offers a different perspective from the previous three friends. He is younger and more assertive, claiming to speak on behalf of God. Elihu emphasizes the importance of humility, acknowledging that suffering can serve a purpose in refining one's character and drawing them closer to God. He represents the voice of wisdom and spiritual insight, encouraging Job to trust in God's plan and sovereignty, although his perspective can often be described as a know-it-all with a heightened perceived sense of one who is speaking on God's behalf.

These four friends symbolize various aspects of human nature and responses to suffering that are still relevant in our lives today. Eliphaz, Bildad, and Zophar represent common tendencies to judge, condemn, and attribute suffering to personal fault or divine punishment. Their perspectives remind us of the dangers of legalism, self-righteousness, and lack of empathy when encountering those in distress.

On the other hand, Elihu's approach highlights the importance of humility, empathy, and spiritual discernment in times of trial. His character serves as a reminder of the value of listening, understanding, and offering comfort rather than jumping to conclusions or passing judgment.

The presence of these four friends in the story of Job serves as a timeless reflection of the complexities of human nature and the diverse ways people respond to suffering, inviting us to reflect on our own attitudes and behaviors when faced with trials. If we read Job's story as a parable, these different responses to Job's suffering can be seen as different ways we respond to our own suffering. For example, some people may lack empathy for themselves when they suffer ("this is all my fault"). Often we have an easier time understanding others' suffering, but have a much more difficult time forgiving ourselves when we have made poor choices or mistakes. We have a tendency to punish ourselves at greater lengths.

Every day that we live, we are also dying at the same time, so in a sense, we grieve and lose part of ourselves daily. When we lose a loved one or a job, or even face the end of a loving relationship, we can often lose our identity because our identity may have been entangled, for better or worse, in that person, job, or relationship. If we can learn to grieve well, to allow God to be God in the midst of our suffering, to refuse the wounded demands of our emotional pain that we should surrender control and give up, then we can minimize the effects of depression, reducing both the severity and the duration of suffering. If we grieve well, if we welcome the comfort of the Holy Spirit, there will be an end to our suffering.

On the other hand, if we allow our anxiety to take over, it prolongs the process, feeding and growing on the hurt, trapping us in despair. An honest acknowledgment of pain and a healthy grieving process centered on God and our true identity in Him is how we can start to move past our own losses.

Grief is a complex and individual process that people go through when they experience a loss. The stages of grief, as outlined by psychiatrist Elisabeth Kübler-Ross, are commonly known as denial, anger, bargaining, depression, and acceptance. While these stages are not necessarily linear and can overlap or be revisited, they provide a framework for understanding and navigating the grieving process.

Examples of Job's suffering as it relates to grief include the loss of his wealth, the loss of his health, and the deaths of his children. Job's grief is palpable as he mourns the devastating losses in his life and struggles to find meaning in his suffering. Through his journey, Job exemplifies the complexities of grief and the resilience of the human spirit in the face of immense hardship. The initial grieving stage of denial involves disbelief and shock, where individuals may struggle to accept the reality of the loss. To apply this stage daily in our lives, it's important to acknowledge and validate our feelings of denial without judging ourselves. It's okay to give ourselves time to come to terms with difficult truths. Initially, Job struggles to accept the tragedies that befall him. He questions why he is facing such hardships and refuses to believe that this is happening to him.

As the reality of the loss sets in, feelings of anger and frustration may surface. It's important to express and process these emotions in healthy ways, such as through journaling, talking to a trusted friend, or engaging in physical activity. By allowing ourselves to feel and release anger, we can keep it from festering and causing further distress. Job expressed his anger toward God, questioning why he was being punished despite being a righteous man. He laments his suffering and demands answers for his pain.

In the stage of bargaining, individuals may try to negotiate with a higher power or seek ways to reverse or mitigate the loss. To apply this stage daily, we can focus on practicing self-compassion and finding constructive ways to cope with feelings of helplessness. Engaging in activities that bring comfort and solace can help us navigate this stage effectively. Job attempts to make sense of his suffering by bargaining with God. He questions whether there is a reason for his pain and seeks to understand the purpose behind his trials.

In the fourth stage—depression—as the full weight of the loss is felt, feelings of sadness, loneliness, and despair may arise. It's important to acknowledge these emotions and seek support from loved ones or a mental health professional if needed. By allowing ourselves to grieve and process our feelings of depression, we can move toward healing and acceptance. Job experiences deep sadness and despair as he grapples with the weight of his suffering. He struggles to find solace and feels overwhelmed by his circumstances.

The final stage involves coming to terms with the loss and integrating it into our lives. To apply this stage daily, we can focus on practicing self-care, setting boundaries, and finding meaning in our experiences. By embracing acceptance, we can honor our feelings and experiences while moving forward with resilience and strength. Ultimately, Job comes to accept his suffering and finds peace in his faith. He acknowledges the limitations of his human understanding and surrenders to God's will, finding a sense of peace amidst his trials.

Incorporating these stages of grief into our daily lives involves being compassionate toward ourselves, seeking support when needed, and allowing ourselves to feel and process our emotions. By acknowledging and navigating the complexities of grief, we can cultivate self-awareness, resilience, and healing in the face of loss. This journey through grief is unique to each individual, and there is no set timeline for when one may move through these stages. It is essential to be patient and gentle with ourselves as we navigate the ups and downs of the grieving process. Remember that healing is not linear, and it is okay to have good days and bad days.

Additionally, it can be helpful to engage in activities that bring comfort and peace during this time. Whether it's spending time in nature, practicing mindfulness and meditation, or engaging in creative outlets, finding moments of solace can aid in the healing process. Ultimately, by embracing the stages of grief and allowing ourselves to feel and process our emotions, we can gradually find a sense of peace and acceptance in the midst of loss. Through self-compassion, self-care, and seeking support from others, we can navigate the complexities of grief and emerge stronger and more resilient on the other side.

A note about supporting others who are grieving: When people see others grieving, the standard phrase seems to be, "We'll be praying for you, brother." But what those suffering truly need is support and some real interactions.

> *"Then the Lord answered Job*
> *out of the whirlwind."*
> —JOB 38:1

What whirlwind? Most likely this is a metaphor for the turmoil and turbulence of Job's life. For the next three chapters, God gives Job a lesson on perspective. As Elihu had pointed out two chapters earlier:

> *"Surely God is great, and we do not know Him;*
> *the number of his years is unsearchable."*
> —JOB 36:26

Why would God put Job through such torment even though he knew his faithful servant would not waver? Surely the God of Heaven can't be goaded into a wager using one of His children? Did the Lord of Creation feel like He had something to prove? Why didn't He simply tell Satan to pull his head in and mind his business? The problem with these questions is that they are human questions stemming from finite brains with limited understanding. As we will see, this is one of the main teaching points of the Book of Job. Who are we to question God? How can we understand Him?

Finally, in Chapter 42, Job repented with the following words:

> *"I had heard of you by the hearing of the ear,*
> *but now my eye sees you; therefore I despise myself,*
> *and repent in dust and ashes."*
> —JOB 42:5–6

The main reason Job ends up repenting was he finally realized that during his grieving he also became self-righteous, believing he did not truly deserve what he was going through. Although that was true—he may not have truly deserved his suffering—his repentance came when he realized his sanctimonious ideals.

Job's friends were humiliated by God's rebuke of their words and conduct during Job's ordeal, and to top it all off, Job's fortunes were restored. After he prayed for his friends, the Lord gave Job twice what he had before.

> *"And the Lord restored the fortunes of Job when he had prayed for his friends; and the Lord gave Job twice as much as he had before. Then there came to him all his brothers and sisters and all who had known him before, and they ate bread with him in his house; they showed him sympathy and comforted him for all the evil that the Lord had brought upon him; and each of them gave him a piece of money and a gold ring. The Lord blessed the latter days of Job more than his beginning; and he had fourteen thousand sheep, six thousand camels, a thousand yoke of oxen, and a thousand donkeys. He also had seven sons and three daughters."*
>
> —JOB 42:10–13

The true meaning of the story of Job lies in the themes of trust, resilience, and the importance of faith in the face of adversity. It serves as a reminder that even in the darkest of times, it is possible to find strength and hope through faith and trust in God. Ultimately, Job's story teaches us that trials and tribulations are a part of life, but it is how we respond to them that defines our character. By remaining faithful and trusting in God, we can overcome even the most difficult challenges and emerge stronger on the other side.

Chapter 5

ABRAHAM AND SARAH

A BETRAYAL OF IMPROBABLE PROPORTIONS

Two hundred and fifty years after the fall of the Tower of Babel, people were still dealing with the fallout of the social upheaval caused by the confusion of language, which was God's response to their haughty, self-aggrandizing efforts to build a tower to Heaven.

Based on the biblical timeline, Abraham's story starts around 1950 BC. It was a chaotic time as people were still recovering from the isolation caused by not being able to communicate with one another. Social connections were severed, and the means of building new connections and relationships with one another were radically altered by the confusion of language with which God cursed the earth. It can also be said that along with the new languages came new beliefs. Although it was counterproductive, people on earth had also separated themselves from God and were believing in and practicing more mystical ways of worship, which, in turn, led to idol worship. People's religious beliefs were compromised.

Abraham was born into this world in which the aftershocks of a cultural earthquake were still being experienced. God chose Abraham to be the man to build a bridge of reconciliation. The one who could help restore His relationship with mankind during tumultuous times. In fact, God appeared to Abraham no less than four separate times, each time promising to make a great nation of his descendants.

Despite these repeated promises, Abraham often resorted to his own methods and relied on his own abilities. He also tried to control many outcomes himself, thinking he knew better than God. Unfortunately for him and those around him, he was wrong in every instance. When he allowed God to take control and when he followed God's plan, Abraham was successful. Oftentimes in our own lives, we have a difficult time giving up control. We want to control the outcome. We want to "know" what is going to happen, when, why, and how. God wants us to trust and obey Him. We are called to walk in the light of the knowledge of the truth, to be led by the Spirit of God. We have been chosen, despite our flaws and failures, to walk by faith, not by sight. This means two things: first, that we continue to trust and obey God irrespective of how things look, and second, that we accept the truth that our sovereign God is in control. As Abraham's story clearly shows us, the good news is that even if we get it wrong, God's grace is sufficient. His plan and His perfect purpose include contingencies covering all our weaknesses, errors, and sins.

The love that Isaac and Ishmael—Abraham's sons—had for their father was unconditional, despite Abraham sometimes placing conditions on others for the reciprocation of love and care. As we delve into Abraham and Sarah's story, one notable aspect that stands out is how often Abraham strayed from following God's plan. In numerous instances, Abraham relied on his own judgment and decisions rather than adhering to God's instructions. Additionally, Sarah's beauty is mentioned, and it seems that Abraham's poor decision-making throughout his life may have been influenced by feelings of inadequacy. Perhaps he felt that he didn't measure up to the same standards as his wife, or maybe he lacked confidence in his own ability to make sound decisions. This lack of self-assurance became evident as he made choices without fully considering the consequences.

Indeed, Abraham's lack of self-confidence and his desire for validation and security could have played a role in his tendency to seek control over the outcomes of his relationships by placing conditions on those he loved. This could have been a way for Abraham to feel a sense of worth and control over his own life, even if it came at the expense of others. By setting conditions, Abraham may have hoped to ensure that his loved ones would reciprocate his love and care, providing him with a sense of reassurance and stability. However, it is important to note that this behavior may have stemmed from his personal struggles and insecurities, rather than reflecting his true love for others.

Abraham was named Abram at birth. Abram, which means "God (or Father) is Exalted," was clearly destined for greatness. Aged seventy-five and living in Haran, the land of his fathers, Abram was called by God to leave his homeland for good.

> *"Now the Lord said to Abram, 'Go from your country and your kindred and your father's house to the land that I will show you. I will make of you a great nation, and I will bless you,*

> *and make your name great, so that you will be a blessing.*
> *I will bless those who bless you, and the one who*
> *curses you I will curse; and in you all the families*
> *of the earth shall be blessed.'"*
>
> —Genesis 12:1–3

Abram obeyed despite the shock and anxiety he must have felt. The whole family was to take everything they owned and move. Moving is stressful and takes a great deal of planning and work, as I am sure we can all relate to on some level. Imagine moving your extended family's houses at the same time. Abram didn't just move his immediate family unit. Everything and everyone were transported to a foreign land, away from safety and familiarity, and Abram was the one in charge. Abram's obedience to God's call is rightly lauded as an act of greatness, but surely we've never fully appreciated what a massive demonstration of humility it was. What vision Abram must have had to get up and leave everything to start anew. What trust! What faith! After all, Abraham is repeatedly mentioned in the New Testament as an example of faith.

> *"For what does the scripture say? 'Abraham believed God, and it was reckoned to him as righteousness.'"*
>
> —Romans 4:3

Even though the promise was grand, Abram must have felt conflicted. He was seventy years old and childless, but God was pledging to make him the father of nations. Like us all, he stumbled by heeding voices other than God's, perhaps the doubts of others or even Sarai. (Sarah's original name was Sarai.) What did people think of Abram's leadership? How often did he doubt himself? In Abram's actions, we hear echoes of the serpent's deception in Eden: "Did God really say that?" God knew Abram's struggles to trust His promise. Abram had to believe, even without understanding how it would happen. His faith wavered at times, like when he asked Sarai (meaning my princess or princess of one family) to pretend to be his sister in Egypt (Genesis 12:10–13). Whether a careful plan or a hasty decision, it backfired. Sometimes our faith falters when survival is at stake. As Christians, do we trust our own abilities when tested, instead of keeping faith in God?

Whether Abram thought out his plan to pass off his wife as his sister or rashly embraced it on the spur of the moment, it was a dumb decision, which was proved by subsequent events. Sometimes, our unwavering faith can be shaken when faced with compromising circumstances. As church members and Christians, when our faith is tested, we may inadvertently rely on our own abilities instead of trusting in God. Consider Abram's emotional turmoil—years of waiting for a child, unsure of his legacy, alone in a strange land. Irrational thoughts can lead to irrational decisions.

Despite God's knowledge of Abram's actions, Sarai remained barren. Fleeing to Egypt to escape famine, Abram and Sarai found themselves in spiritually challenging circumstances, adding to their already difficult situation.

Imagine the following conversation between the husband and wife: *Sarai, once we get into Egypt, you may have to pretend to be my sister. Because if you don't, the Pharaoh may kill me and take you if he finds out you are my wife. He too will see how beautiful you are and want you for himself. So, it will be just easier for both of us if you tell him you are my sister.* That message to Sarai must have hurt worse than any starvation she would have faced back home. How was Abram's plan going to work? Surely he would have more success with honesty. Why would he ask her to lie for him, and would it really be safer or easier?

If Abram had remained faithful and trusted in God's protection, he would not have had to lie about his relationship with his wife. Pharaoh was tricked into believing that Sarai was single, so he took her for himself. Of course he did. Why wouldn't he? He was the Pharaoh of Egypt, and if he wanted something, he was sure to get it. Abram's foolish and misguided attempt to protect his wife resulted in him losing her, and once she was gone, he was powerless to do anything about it. During some of the time that Abram and Sarai spent in Egypt, Sarai stayed with Pharaoh. Imagine the emotional trauma she must have gone through, and her sense of abandonment. Her God-fearing husband, the man who was destined to become the father of many nations, had promised to protect her, but had failed.

Sarai's perspective often gets lost in those early years of their relationship because of the understandable focus on Abram. However, keep in mind that Hagar, who would become the first woman to bear a child for Abram, was an Egyptian slave, likely given to Sarai when she was in Egypt. Is it possible that the Pharaoh gave Hagar to Sarai while Sarai was staying at the palace? And who is to say that Sarai and the Pharaoh did not have a sexual relationship, considering he thought she was a single woman? It is only natural to ponder the issue of Sarai's inability to conceive. Sarai continued to be childless until she reached the age of ninety. Had Sarai conceived a child with the Pharaoh, it would have contradicted God's intention for Abram to be the patriarch of a mighty nation. Her barrenness was undeniably a part of God's divine plan.

And the only other person to know that secret of a potential relationship between Sarai and Pharaoh was Hagar. In any case, God was displeased with what Abram did, but interestingly chose to punish Pharaoh rather than Abram.

Some modern readers of the Bible consider this to be unfair, but who are we to question God? Perhaps, in his infinite wisdom, God felt Abram had suffered enough. Imagine the torment of knowing Sarai had become the Pharaoh's property. Furthermore, God may have had other reasons for afflicting Pharaoh. God's punishment was to inflict plagues on Pharaoh's household, but once Pharaoh found out, surely suspecting the disaster was not a coincidence, he told Abram to leave immediately.

> *"'Why did you say, "She is my sister," so that I took her for my wife? Now then, here is your wife, take her, and be gone.' And Pharaoh gave men orders concerning him; and they set him on the way, with his wife and all that he had."*
> —GENESIS 12:19–20

Until the truth came out, Abram was well looked after and grew wealthier. His riches accumulated courtesy of Pharaoh's favor. Was that some kind of compensation? A payoff for Sarai? Was Pharaoh acting out of guilt or generosity?

After the Egypt debacle, Abram and Sarai's relationship was damaged. There is no doubt of that. But with time, perhaps the couple was able to come to terms with what happened, and Sarai forgave her husband for what he did. Either that, or she harbored a deep resentment, which was to be later revealed in what some would consider an act of revenge.

After Sarai was returned to Abram and they were booted out of Egypt, God appeared to Abram again, in a vision this time.

> *"After these things the word of the Lord came to Abram in a vision, 'Do not be afraid, Abram, I am your shield; your reward shall be very great.'"*
> —Genesis 15:1

God spoke with him to reassure Abram, who wondered not only how he was going to become a father of a nation when he was childless, but whether he had disqualified himself by his fearful and fateful decision to abandon his wife. He somewhat humorously made the point that his only heir was a Syrian from Damascus. It didn't add up in Abram's mind, yet in verse 4 of chapter 15, God gave it to him straight.

> *"But the word of the Lord came to him, 'This man shall not be your heir; no one but your very own issue shall be your heir.' He brought him outside and said, 'Look toward heaven and count the stars, if you are able to count them.' Then he said to him, 'So shall your descendants be.' And he believed the Lord; and the Lord reckoned it to him as righteousness."*
> —Genesis 15:4–6

Abram was affirmed and renewed in his faith, but Sarai was not convinced that she was necessarily going to be the one to fulfill God's promise to Abram by bearing him a child. Either from doubt, or as an act of revenge, or even as a genuine misinterpretation of what God had said, Sarai told Abram to sleep with her Egyptian maid, Hagar. That in itself was not unusual from a cultural point of view. Polygamy was an accepted practice among the foreigners whose land Abram and his family were traveling through. The idea of having sex with multiple partners in one household was not strange. What is strange, or at least questionable, was Abram's decision to go along with Sarai's plan. We could give him the benefit of the doubt and say that he too was misinterpreting God's promise of an heir, but it appears to be another demonstration of his impatience and lack of trust.

Naturally, Hagar's pregnancy made Sarai jealous, which caused tension between the three of them. It is obvious that Abram was trying to please his wife instead of doing the right thing by Hagar and his unborn child. His first. His heir. The one he had dreamed of for so long. This led to Sarai banishing Hagar while she was pregnant. Abram condoned the action, but he was also dealing with the guilt of sleeping with Hagar, even though Sarai told him to. It is almost as if their roles from their time in Egypt had flipped.

Hagar did not have any say. As a slave, she had no rights and had to do as she was told. As soon as it became known that Hagar was with child, Sarai began mistreating her, according to Genesis 16:4–6. Neither Sarai nor Hagar could have been totally comfortable with what was happening. One can only imagine how Sarai must have felt. She was the one who was supposed to produce a son for Abram, and even though it was her doing, now Hagar was pregnant. Sarai's sadness, her disappointment, and the shame she must have felt at not being able to have children must have made her truly wretched. Her feelings, however, did not justify the mistreatment of Hagar.

Abram was 86 years old when Hagar gave birth to his son, whom he named Ishmael. Hagar returned to the camp, and things seemed to settle down, but Abram had gone off plan again. Fifteen years later, God appeared a third time to repeat his promise to Abram, whom he renamed Abraham, which means "father of a multitude" or "father of a nation."

> *"When Abram was ninety-nine years old, the Lord appeared to Abram, and said to him, 'I am God Almighty; walk before me, and be blameless. And I will make my covenant between me and you, and will make you exceedingly numerous.' Then Abram fell on his face; and God said to him, 'As for me, this is my covenant with you: You shall be the ancestor of a multitude of nations. No longer shall your name be Abram, but your name shall be Abraham; for I have made you the ancestor of a multitude of nations. I will make you exceedingly fruitful; and I will make nations of you, and kings shall come from you. I will establish my covenant between me and you, and your offspring after you throughout their generations, for an everlasting covenant, to be God to you and to your offspring after you. And I will give to you, and to your offspring after you, the land where you are now an alien, all the land of Canaan, for a perpetual holding; and I will be their God.'"*
>
> —Genesis 17:1–8

From then on, Abraham carried God's promise in his new name. Sarai was also given a new name—Sarah, meaning "mother of nations."

Two broken people with deep shame and guilt were given new names—given a fresh start, a second chance. They were reminded of God's promise, His plan to build a great nation that would lead to the birth of the greatest King, Jesus. How did the newly named Abraham and Sarah react? One-hundred-year-old Abraham laughed at God's suggestion that he and his ninety-year-old wife would have a child.

Unsurprisingly, God was not bothered by Abraham's reaction. He said nothing about Abraham's attitude, or about his past failings, but instead confirmed His promise and sealed the deal by instituting the practice of circumcision. It was to be for all time a sign of the covenant between God and His people.

Some time after Abraham, Ishmael, and all the males of the tribe recovered from their sacred surgery, God visited Abraham for a fourth time. How many times did God need to visit Abraham for him to truly believe the promise? I don't know about you, but once would be enough for me. Or would it? How easy or how difficult is it for us to accept God's promises? If Jesus were to come to me in person, I wouldn't need any more reminders to stay on track. Or would I?

This fourth visit is particularly special because God appeared to Abraham as three men. Modern readers may interpret this as a manifestation of the Holy Trinity.

> *"The Lord appeared to Abraham by the oaks of Mamre,*
> *as he sat at the entrance of his tent in the heat of the day.*
> *He looked up and saw three men standing near him.*
> *When he saw them, he ran from the tent entrance to*
> *meet them, and bowed down to the ground."*
>
> —Genesis 18:1–2

They spoke to Abraham as one, accepting his offer of hospitality. God said he would return to them in about one year, at which time Sarah would have borne a son, the child of the promise. This time, Sarah laughed at the suggestion, but was rebuked by God, who said in Genesis 18:14, *"Is anything too wonderful for the Lord?"* Ironically, the name Isaac means "one who laughs or rejoices." Sarah laughed at the idea of having a child at almost ninety; however, she would also rejoice.

Later, Abraham traveled further south to Gerar, where he inexplicably repeated his Egyptian mistake by tricking the king of Gerar, Abimelech, into believing Sarah was his sister, instead of just saying she was his wife. It would be nice to think Abraham learned from his mistake the first time, but he again stumbled and repeated the error he had made just years before. Imagine the wounds that were once again opened when Sarah was presented to the king as Abraham's sister. The years of healing. The moments of forgiveness. Everything came flooding back again when that wound was viciously reopened. How could Abraham make the same grave mistake a second time? How can we make that same mistake a second, third, fourth time? Yet we do, and are indeed at times the embodiment of the fool in Proverbs who is likened to a dog returning to its own vomit when he repeats his folly (Proverbs 26:11).

So, Abimelech took Sarah, just like Pharaoh had, but God visited Abimelech in a dream and told him the truth. When the king confronted Abraham, Abraham gave the same excuse for lying about Sarah.

> *"Abraham said, 'I did it because I thought, There is no fear of God at all in this place, and they will kill me because of my wife.'"*
> —Genesis 20:11

Where did Abraham's fear come from? After all that he had been through, why did he choose to lie and abandon his wife again? Even more remarkable than Abraham's failure, his pusillanimity, his descent into fear and anxiety—greater than all that was God's grace. After Abraham confesses his lie, which he can't deny, Abimelech gives Sarah back to him, then showers him with gifts and lays out a welcome mat for Abraham and his family.

> *"Then Abimelech took sheep and oxen,*
> *and male and female slaves, and gave them to*
> *Abraham, and restored his wife Sarah to him.*
> *Abimelech said, 'My land is before you; settle where it*
> *pleases you.' To Sarah he said, 'Look, I have given your brother*
> *a thousand pieces of silver; it is your exoneration before all*
> *who are with you; you are completely vindicated.'"*
> —Genesis 20:14–16

Abraham showed many signs of uncertainty, often questioning himself about what was happening in his life. Even though God told him multiple times to be patient and just be present, he attempted to do things his way. Time and time again, God assured Abraham that He would do great things for him and through him, yet over and over Abraham failed to accept his place in God's plan.

Abraham's self-doubt and need for control impacted not only his relationship with God, but his relationship with Sarah. Sarah's journey was paved with times of uncertainty, frustration, discouragement, and betrayal, often due to Abraham's decisions. However, it was also marked with joy, laughter, and an undeniable faith in God. Sarah's presence in the biblical narratives and history was so significant that she stands out as the only woman whose age is explicitly mentioned in the Bible. According to Genesis 23:1, Sarah passed away at the age of 127, leaving a lasting legacy on the pages of scripture.

However, coupled with Abraham's uncertainty is his love, particularly in his relationships with his family. His love for Sarah, Isaac, and Ishmael is evident throughout the biblical narrative, despite the challenges and difficult decisions he faced. Overall, Abraham's emotional state was complex and multifaceted, characterized by a deep faith in God, moments of fear and uncertainty, a steadfast hope in God's promises, and a strong love for his family. Abraham is still credited as the person we can—and should—look to as an example of strong faith.

Chapter 6

HAGAR AND ISHMAEL

THE RESILIENCE OF A SINGLE MOTHER

As we read in the previous chapter, Hagar played a pivotal role in Abram and Sarai's life. It's worth exploring the role Hagar played in Ishmael's life and his development into a father of many nations as well. In the thirty years I've been attending church and listening to preachers speak from the pulpit, I cannot recall a single message specifically focused on Hagar. Yet, after my analysis of her, I discovered a very powerful and amazing woman: an Egyptian slave who went from a life of servitude to raising a son, a child fathered by Abraham (Abram). Ishmael, whose name means "God will hear," became the father of Islam. We will come back to him later in the chapter, but let's start with Hagar.

Hagar was a slave whom Pharaoh gave to Sarai when she and Abram were told to leave Egypt, or possibly before that, during Sarai's time in the palace. Hagar remained faithful to Sarai throughout her time of service. In a rush to fulfill God's promise about her husband becoming the father of many nations, and unable to fall pregnant herself, Sarai tells Abram to have a child with Hagar.

> *"And Sarai said to Abram, 'You see that the Lord has prevented me from bearing children; go in to my slave-girl; it may be that I shall obtain children by her.' And Abram listened to the voice of Sarai."*
> —Genesis 16:2

It is important to note that Sarai is looking to Hagar as a means to bear a child that Sarai can raise. If Hagar knew the real intention of this plan—Hagar getting pregnant but only for Sarai to call the child her own—it is no surprise that when Hagar found out she was pregnant, she began to despise her mistress, Sarai (verse 4). Surrogacy is a beautiful gift to give a couple trying to conceive, but I don't believe this was the case. Being a slave, Hagar didn't go into this contract to bless the couple with a child for them to raise as their own. She was forced into conceiving a child she would have to give up.

When Hagar first felt those flutters of life growing inside her, I can only imagine the bittersweet pain she felt. The joy of growing a life and the excitement of awaiting the birth of your child, only to be forced to give the child to someone else to raise. She may have fancied Abram, may even have enjoyed their coupling, and perhaps, as a result of this opportunity, began to dream of a better life for herself and her offspring. On the other hand, she may have dreaded the thought of sleeping with Abram and may have feared the consequences. How could it not cause problems between her and Sarai? We don't know how she felt about the whole ordeal, but the point is she had no choice.

The child would be Sarai's. Hagar was just a means to the end goal of making Abram a father of many nations. Once again, she was reminded of her value in life—a slave to fulfill the needs of those in control of her. She was there to serve and do what she was told. But being forced to bear a child only to give them up? Now that crossed the line.

Sarai recognized the hurt she caused Hagar when she told Abram that Hagar despised her (Genesis 16:5). However, Sarai still tried to place blame on Abram, telling him it was all his fault. At this point, Abram probably felt caught up in all the emotional drama between the two women and just wanted it to end. You could probably slice the tension in the air whenever the two women were in the same room. This had to create a very uncomfortable atmosphere in their home. The Bible tells us that when Hagar became pregnant, she began to look at Sarai with contempt. *"He went in to Hagar, and she conceived; and when she saw that she had conceived, she looked with contempt on her mistress"* (Genesis 16:4). Given her status as a slave, it was unwise of Hagar to goad Sarai that way, and we can understand that with an already heavy emotional load on Sarai, Hagar pushed her over the edge. Naturally, Sarai complained to Abram, who washed his hands of the problem by telling her, *"Your slave-girl is in your power; do to her as you please"* (Genesis 16:6).

Hagar fled into the wilderness and was camped by a spring when the Angel of the Lord approached her. In Genesis 16:7–14, we read about the interesting conversation that followed. Hagar was at a very low point in her life: a slave; pregnant; away from her family, friends, and community—all alone. A woman who had no control of her life and was told what to do all day, every day. Even when she did everything asked of her, she was still mistreated. People often hurt others, sometimes deliberately, because they cannot accept or deal with their own personal problems. They either can't or won't take responsibility for the consequences of their actions. In Hagar's case, Sarai was abusing her, treating her without respect or any kindness, and Abram had abandoned her.

Abram and Sarai were meant to be good examples of a God-fearing man and woman. That is not the impression readers of this story are left with, nor would Hagar have seen any goodness in the behavior of her master and mistress.

The Angel of God called out to Hagar by name and asked where she came from. Interestingly and surprisingly, Hagar did not run away from the Angel. There is nothing to suggest in the biblical account that she was afraid. Perhaps she was so dejected, she was beyond caring. It is likely she was depressed, and she was certainly fearful, but not of God, it seems. The Angel appeared to her at a time when she had no one else; she had hit rock bottom. She was ready for a miracle, and God provided one.

Hagar told the Angel that she was running away from Sarai. The Angel listened, then simply told Hagar to go back to her mistress. Imagine Hagar's disappointment to have received the honor of a miraculous visit by an angel only to be commanded to go back to the very horrors she had fled. Surely she would have received these words as unfair—a further injustice, and a cruel one at that. God knew exactly what Hagar had been through, and what further mistreatment she would go through, but He sent her back. If it sounds awful to us, how much worse must it have been for Hagar? However, the instructions are followed by a promise and a prophecy.

> *"And the angel of the Lord said to her,*
> *'Now you have conceived and shall bear a son;*
> *you shall call him Ishmael, for the Lord has given heed to*
> *your affliction. He shall be a wild ass of a man, with his hand*
> *against everyone, and everyone's hand against him;*
> *and he shall live at odds with all his kin.' So she named the Lord*
> *who spoke to her, 'You are El-roi'; for she said, 'Have I really*
> *seen God and remained alive after seeing him?'"*
>
> —Genesis 16:11–13

That personal visit from the Angel of the Lord and the prophetic words that recognized and appreciated her suffering were enough to strengthen Hagar and give her the courage to return to her abhorrent life in Abram's camp. She acknowledged God and finally felt as though she had been seen as a person by someone. After so much rejection, Hagar was finally accepted, and by none other than God Himself. Prior to their conversation, this woman did not feel valued, or that she belonged anywhere. Now she felt encouraged and seen by God Almighty.

It's interesting to reflect on that conversation. Hagar remained calm and interacted with God like she was talking to a friend and telling him all of her problems. The Angel of God could be perceived as a pre-incarnate of Jesus. Imagine if we could just talk to Jesus as a friend rather than saying the type of overly sentimental prayer that we often hear in a church setting. The conversation was also remarkable because Hagar is one of only five women who had a conversation with God in the Old Testament. Eve, Sarah, Rebekah, and Deborah were the other women to have the honor of conversing with God. God spoke to Hagar—a pagan unbeliever, a slave, disregarded by society, disrespected, mistreated by her mistress, a nobody. That's pretty cool.

Remember, Hagar was at her lowest point in life: homeless, pregnant, no family, no direction or perceived purpose, and no provisions (food or money). She most likely felt lost, saddened, abandoned, frustrated, and resentful over the way she had been treated. Yet, it is clear Hagar was chosen by God. The fact that God told Hagar to go back to Sarai could only mean He was not done with her. He was preparing her or rather molding her into the woman and mother she must become to Ishmael, and to the many nations that would call her son "Father."

Hagar's situation was still very complicated. In the first place, it was unlikely that Hagar's living conditions would improve when she returned to Sarai's service. God didn't tell her that He would make everything okay. He didn't say anything about healing the rift between the two women, or about healing the hurt. Furthermore, God told Hagar that Ishmael was not going to have an easy life either. He would need a strong mother figure to teach and prepare him for his journey. Hagar's suffering strengthened her for that task. She obeyed God and went straight back into the furnace of her horrific circumstances. However, she felt empowered by God's grace and power.

We see how God's sovereign plan is larger than we can imagine and understand. Abram and Sarai's life would have been very different if they had faithfully followed God's instructions in the same way that Hagar did in that moment.

Ishmael was born when Abram was eighty-six years old, and both he and his mother continued to suffer mistreatment in Abram's house. Fourteen years later, Sarah became pregnant, just as God said she would, but after her son, Isaac, was born, she told Abraham to force Hagar and Ishmael to leave because she did not want Ishmael to get any of their fortune.

> *"The child grew, and was weaned; and Abraham made a great feast on the day that Isaac was weaned. But Sarah saw the son of Hagar the Egyptian, whom she had borne to Abraham, playing with her son Isaac. So she said to Abraham, 'Cast out this slave woman with her son; for the son of this slave woman shall not inherit along with my son Isaac.'"*
> —Genesis 21:8–10

It pained Abraham greatly because he loved his son Ishmael, but God assured him that He would look after them, so Abraham got some bread and water for Hagar and Ishmael and sent them on their way. Abraham had all the riches in the world. He had plenty of money, animals, and slaves. He could have ignored the inevitable protests from Sarah and given Ishmael and his mother much more, or at least enough to get them safely to another location or even send Hagar back to Egypt. Abraham could have sent some of his men and donkeys to help Hagar and Ishmael on their journey. He could have instructed his men to ensure Hagar and Ishmael were safely settled in another town. However, he only gave them a loaf of bread and a skin of water. This, unfortunately, is a perfect example of a man not providing for his family. After all, it was supposed to be Abraham's responsibility to provide for Hagar and Ishmael. Instead, he gave in to Sarah's wishes and essentially signed a death warrant for his son.

This moment must have also left a lasting effect on Ishmael. His father sent him and Hagar away when they had done nothing wrong.

He was probably between the ages of thirteen and fifteen when he was forced out of his own father's house. During that confusing time, and the general emotional mayhem of adolescence, Ishmael was without a father, and Sarah was essentially responsible for that. Ishmael was seen as a threat by Sarah, a threat that she needed to remove and a threat young Ishmael would not have understood even if he had been told. So, once more, Hagar was forced into the isolation of the wilderness, but this time she had a child with her. The food and water ran out quickly. Mother and son were doomed to die in the desert.

> *"Then she went and sat down opposite him a good way off, about the distance of a bowshot; for she said, 'Do not let me look on the death of the child.' And as she sat opposite him, she lifted up her voice and wept."*
> —Genesis 21:16

God once again appeared to Hagar as Ishmael was dying a slow death. He spoke with Hagar and encouraged her, repeating and confirming the promise He made to her when they last spoke. God provided water and a safe place for them to rest, and so they survived by the mercy of God. Hagar and Ishmael eventually settled in a new town and began their life, and when he was of age, Hagar found a wife for Ishmael.

Ishmael grew and developed but would have had some problems during his formative years. I'm sure he had abandonment and trust issues due to the way Abraham and Sarah had treated him. However, with the resilience demonstrated to him by his mother, who also nurtured him through their experiences together, he grew strong. Ishmael did indeed go on to become a father of many nations.

My original intent was to write a behavioral analysis of Ishmael. However, once I started analyzing his story, I could not overlook the more powerful individual in the narrative: Hagar. Ishmael's survival, development, and upbringing were attributed to a woman who converted from being a pagan to following God. She went from being a slave to being the mother of a man who would also become a father of many nations. Because of Hagar's commitment to God and raising Ishmael, the father of the Islamic faith was allowed to live a full life rather than die in a desert.

The idea of single motherhood is a topic rarely, if ever, discussed in any given church setting. Single mothers can be and are powerful in ways not often discussed in the Christian faith. The unfortunate reality I've witnessed is how women's roles are often diminished within churches. There seems to be a disconnect at times, when men will make the "executive" decisions but the women of these churches are only made aware of the decisions rather than being empowered to be part of the conversation.

We can't dismiss the role of a maternal figure in a child's development. Most of the stories discussed or taught from the pulpit are about male figures and their accomplishments. Single mothers, like Hagar, deserve praise. Hagar was a woman worthy of respect. She was chosen by God, despite her flaws, even though she was not even of the same faith as the House of Abraham. God called an idol worshiper (what we would call a pagan), and He heard her prayer for deliverance, acknowledged her pain, and strengthened her.

What did Hagar do that was so wrong? Did she deserve the mistreatment she suffered? Single mothers? What have they done wrong? We often make assumptions about people and the situations in which they find themselves. God calls us to show grace and to honor people who, like Hagar, fight the good fight. Against all odds, Hagar kept her faith and followed God's instructions. She raised a son all on her own and worked hard in her life to provide for him. Her resilience was learned by Ishmael, who went on to have a multitude of children and create his wealth because God also had a plan for him.

When life seems at its lowest—and you may be hungry, broke, and homeless, with no family and no friends—don't lose hope. Hagar and Ishmael didn't. When all seems lost, God will come through for you. At just the right time. He will provide for you and ensure you have what you need. We just need to be willing to ask and be prepared to listen.

Chapter 7

ISAAC

OBEDIENCE TO THE FATHER...
THE HEAVENLY FATHER

The rich story of Isaac, a son obedient to his earthly father and faithful to his heavenly Father, holds valuable lessons that resonate through time. While Isaac's obedience to his father was a significant part of his narrative, it is his unwavering faith in God that truly stands out. Despite often being portrayed as the chosen son of Abraham and the father of three major religions, Isaac was not without his flaws, which are often overlooked in discussions. Isaac's story includes instances of deceit, such as when he lied to a king to ensure his safety, even though he had the Almighty on his side. In a cruel twist of fate, a similar deceptive tactic was used against Isaac by one of his own sons.

One of Isaac's most significant flaws was his failure to recognize how he, like his father, Abraham, had abandoned his eldest son, Esau, in the same manner that Abraham had cast out Ishmael. This abandonment of Esau, driven by favoritism toward Jacob, led to a fracture in the family that echoed the rift between Abraham and Ishmael. Despite these shortcomings, God still chose Isaac and bestowed great riches upon him. Interestingly, Isaac's interactions with God differed from those of his father, Abraham, indicating a unique relationship between Isaac and the divine.

Abraham was chosen by God to be the father of many nations, yet he did not live to see the fulfillment of God's promise. Isaac, his son, took over the mantle of Abraham's divinely appointed legacy. We often hear about Isaac as the young man who almost became a human sacrifice at the hands of his father. Oftentimes when Isaac is taught as a lesson in Sunday School, he is referred to as the son who was willing to do anything for his father, even if it meant losing his life. Yet there is rarely any focus on Isaac's human reactions to this situation—either in the moment, or as they reverberated through the rest of his life.

Isaac was cut from the same cloth as Abraham, most likely a kind, loving, patient, and respectful young man. He also followed in his father's footsteps with his relationship to God, with Abraham teaching him not only how to properly serve God, but also the story of their family and God's promise to them. Abraham and Sarah were well over one hundred years old when Isaac was a teenager. That might have been an issue for him as perhaps there was not such an unusually large age gap between his peers and their parents. He must have learned at some point that he had a brother named Ishmael. In all likelihood, he would have had questions about the absence of his brother and would have learned about the circumstances, although we don't know how much his parents told him, or how colored their accounts might have been. It was likely a topic of discussion when the brothers were reunited at Abraham's funeral (Genesis 25:9).

In Genesis 22, we read about a very significant moment in the lives of Abraham and his son Isaac: God commanded Abraham to bring Isaac to a certain place, and offer him up as a "burnt offering" (Genesis 22:2). Isaac was most likely in his late teens to early twenties. Although he was certainly capable of making his own decisions, Isaac still followed Abraham's direction as they climbed the mountain.

> *"Isaac said to his father Abraham, 'Father!' And he said, 'Here I am, my son.' He said, 'The fire and the wood are here, but where is the lamb for a burnt offering?' Abraham said, 'God himself will provide the lamb for a burnt offering, my son.' So the two of them walked on together."*
> —Genesis 22:7–8

Isaac's question was more than reasonable. After all, Abraham had not said anything to Isaac about him being the sacrifice. However, Abraham's response is particularly interesting in the way Abraham must have said, "Here I am, my son." And again calling Isaac "my son" after Abraham had responded. This type of emotionality and use of the term "my son" must have come from a deep place within Abraham, knowing that he would have to sacrifice his long-awaited son and heir. Abraham's tone must have gotten more and more solemn as they climbed the mountain. Imagine if Isaac thought this was going to be a "father and son" camping trip. As they climb the mountain, the reality of the situation for both of them settles in, and the jovial tone turns to somber.

Much of the teaching focus of this story is on Abraham's obedience to God's painful command. However, Isaac must have had numerous fleeting thoughts as he lay upon the altar and the reality finally hit him that he was the one to be sacrificed. Put yourself on that altar. How would you feel? What would you do? Would you have prayed, possibly like Isaac may have? Any rational individual would fight, try to run away, or downright refuse to lie still upon the altar. The fact that he did not fight or run away indicates that Isaac truly loved and trusted his father. Keep in mind that Isaac had most likely witnessed Abraham's faithfulness to God throughout his upbringing. Abraham's testimony also may have created a special bond between God and Isaac. Isaac's faith in God was most likely a direct result of Abraham's service to God as well. At the root of Isaac's obedience to his father was his true faith in God, knowing that God would provide in a timely manner.

Abraham told Isaac that God would provide, which He did in the end, but consider those agonizingly long moments leading up to God's ultimate provision of a ram. See the young man, Isaac, prone and surrendered. See the blade in his father's hand raised high, ready to strike. Even as the knife hovered above him, held firmly in Abraham's trembling hand, Isaac still did not move. God finally called out to Abraham. Think of the relief that may have occurred when a ram appeared in the thickets. The result of this act of obedience by Abraham was that God confirmed His promise to make him the father of many nations (Genesis 22:15–18).

For Isaac, it was an unforgettable lesson in trust, as well as the cost and rewards of obedience. Even though Isaac was saved, almost being sacrificed by his father was a traumatic and life-changing moment. Often the message of Isaac's faithfulness to God gets lost in the translation where Abraham's covenant was renewed. Based on Isaac's behaviors as he was being bound up by Abraham, I believe the reality began to set in that he was going to be the sacrifice. Isaac did not protest. Even as Isaac lay upon the altar, he continued to remain humble before God, knowing that God would save him. Isaac may have even prayed silently because he did not utter any words or plea for salvation when Abraham stood over him holding the knife. God recognized Abraham's obedience. However, I believe God rewarded Isaac for his faithfulness to Him—and part of that reward was a renewed faith in God. Isaac had indisputable proof that God was watching out for him, that he was important to God's plan.

As Isaac was growing up, he was being instructed and taught by his father and his Heavenly Father. God still talked to Isaac and continued to mold him into a strong and faithful man, but Abraham remained a person of tremendous influence in his life. After Sarah died, Abraham made sure Isaac, his son of promise, would marry someone within the family (Genesis 24:1–4). God's hand was all over the meeting of Isaac and Rebekah, who was Abraham's niece. The arranged marriage between the two was never in doubt, and Isaac married her as soon as practicable after she arrived in the Negev, where Isaac had settled (Genesis 24:62–67).

Abraham did not only teach Isaac how to interact with God. We also see Isaac repeat the mistakes of Abraham in his family relationships: passing his wife off as his sister, and showing favoritism to one son over another. A famine occurred, and Isaac and Rebekah traveled south to Gerar because God warned Isaac not to go to Egypt (Genesis 26:2–3). So far, so good for Isaac and Rebekah, until the men of Gerar asked Isaac about her, and inexplicably, just like Abraham had done in Egypt, Isaac told them that Rebekah was his sister. Isaac then appears to have instructed Rebekah to play along so that the people of Gerar would look fondly upon him and not hurt or kill him. If Isaac had heard about what happened with his parents in Egypt, his behavior would have been even more bizarre. If he knew the consequences of Abraham's decision, then why on earth would he do the same thing? It's a replay of a disaster (Genesis 26:6–11). Perhaps we should give Isaac the benefit of the doubt and say that his parents concealed the knowledge of that incident from him. Even then, Isaac's decision appears to be very weak.

Unsurprisingly, the king of that land, Abimelech, was furious when he discovered the truth, and he eventually booted Isaac and his family out of Gerar. (Although this occurred in the same region where Abraham encountered an Abimelech, most likely "Abimelech" was more of a title than a name and meant "Father Our King or My Father Is My King.")

This banishment also carried a blessing because Abimelech told everyone in his kingdom, with an accompanying threat of death, not to lay a finger on Rebekah. Furthermore, Genesis 26:12–14 tells us that the Lord blessed Isaac immeasurably, making him a very wealthy man. Immediately following Isaac's potentially life-threatening mistake, while they were still living in Gerar under the protection of King Abimelech, God blessed him. That is amazing grace. Isaac became so wealthy and powerful in Gerar that finally Abimelech sent them away.

> *"And Abimelech said to Isaac, 'Go away from us;*
> *you have become too powerful for us.'"*
> —Genesis 26:16

We can only hope that Isaac was grateful beyond words for God's kindness to him and his family. Sometime later, God appeared to

Isaac to affirm the promise He made to Abraham. The Lord's choice of words here is very interesting because of the reference to Abraham.

> *"And that very night the Lord appeared*
> *to him and said, 'I am the God of your father Abraham;*
> *do not be afraid, for I am with you and will bless you*
> *and make your offspring numerous for*
> *my servant Abraham's sake.'"*
> —Genesis 26:24

Was God suggesting that Isaac had blown it and the only reason he would be blessed was so that God could be faithful to Abraham? In any case, Isaac responds with an act of worship. He built an altar to the Lord. Even though God was saying that Isaac's prosperity was because of Abraham, not Isaac himself, Isaac responded with worship. Not jealousy or resentment, but worship. Isaac's fluctuating behavior continued to strengthen his bond with God. It seems as though he was slowly unlearning the traits he had picked up from Abraham. Isaac's relationship and faithfulness were truly solidified during the moment he lay upon the altar on top of Mount Moriah. I'm sure Isaac often replayed that moment in his head, recalling what it was like to have almost been sacrificed and remembering that ultimately God provided at the perfect time.

However, this transformation was short-lived, as Isaac eventually reverted back to his old ways. In his old age and blindness, Isaac called on the oldest of his twin sons, Esau, to receive his blessing. What should have been a simple request for a meal turned into a deceitful act orchestrated by Rebekah and the younger twin, Jacob. As we delve into the next chapter, Rebekah and Jacob conspired to trick Isaac into blessing Jacob instead of Esau, the rightful recipient of the blessing.

This act of deception marked a pivotal moment in Isaac's life, as it highlighted the recurring theme of trickery and manipulation within his family. Despite his blindness, Isaac's actions mirrored those of his father Abraham, who had also resorted to deceit in the past. This incident not only strained the relationship between Isaac and Esau but also showcased the complex dynamics within the family.

The consequences of this deception would ripple through generations, shaping the destiny of Isaac's descendants. It was a stark reminder that the apple doesn't fall far from the tree, and that Isaac's struggle to break free from the patterns established by Abraham was far from over.

In examining the parallels between Isaac's treatment of Esau and Abraham's treatment of Ishmael, we can see a pattern of favoritism and neglect that transcends generations. Just as Abraham showed favoritism toward Isaac, his true heir, and ultimately sent Ishmael away, so too did Isaac favor Jacob over Esau, leading to a similar outcome.

Isaac's actions toward Esau reflect a lack of consideration and empathy. When it came time to give his blessing, he chose to bless Jacob, even though he was tricked, instead of Esau, despite Esau being the firstborn. This decision not only caused deep resentment and hurt in Esau, but also perpetuated a cycle of favoritism and division within the family. Furthermore, Isaac's failure to reprimand Rebekah for her deception and manipulation in securing the blessing for Jacob shows a lack of leadership and accountability. By turning a blind eye to Rebekah's actions, Isaac allowed deceit and dishonesty to go unchecked, further eroding the family's trust and unity. In reflecting on Isaac's mistakes, we can see the damaging effects of favoritism, neglect, and lack of communication within a family. By failing to treat Esau with the same respect and consideration as Jacob, Isaac perpetuated a cycle of rivalry and division that ultimately led to estrangement and broken relationships.

Isaac's story serves as a cautionary tale, reminding us of the importance of fairness, empathy, and open communication in our relationships with others. By learning from Isaac's mistakes, we can strive to build stronger, more harmonious relationships based on mutual respect and understanding.

Even though we are the product of our parents, it does not mean that we must repeat their behaviors. As I've taught my son and daughters, I want them to take the best of what their mother and I have taught them and to try to leave the bad behaviors behind. Although at times we find ourselves inherently displaying similar mannerisms or making similar choices as our parents, it does not follow that we are locked into that way of living. Just because we are the product of our parents does not mean that we must turn out like them. It can be challenging; however, it is possible. The cycle can be broken.

I decided when I was about thirteen years old that I did not want to grow up being an alcoholic. I had lost several family members to the addiction and had been raised in a home with plenty of domestic abuse. Alcohol ran rampant in our household. I had seen the devastation and pain it caused, and I did not want to have the same affliction. I made a conscious decision to never drink alcohol. Now in my late forties, I have toasted many friends at special occasions, but I have never truly been under the influence of alcohol or drugs for the fear that I may become addicted. I did not want to repeat the same behavior as my cousins, uncles, brothers, and father. That was a choice I made.

Perhaps you want to make a similar choice to break the chains of the past, to not repeat the flaws of your parents. Some of you may want to do that, to make that decision right now, but you are wondering how you can follow through. You wonder if you have the strength to do it. Jesus Christ offers new life to those who surrender to Him. New life means exactly that. A fresh start. A never-ending series of "second chances." A promise to always be with you and, if you allow it, a dramatic transformation from the inside out. The new life Jesus offers includes the power to make good choices. The ball is in your court.

Chapter 8

JACOB AND ESAU

LIFE'S SCARS CAN BE DECEIVING

If ever there was a portentous pregnancy and birth in the Bible other than that of Christ, the birth of Rebekah's twins, Jacob and Esau, is surely it. It was a miraculous conception and a difficult pregnancy, so much so that Rebekah went to the Lord in despair, wondering how she could endure such pain and asking about the purpose of her suffering. It's probably the most common prayer of all time: *why is this happening to me?*

> *"The children struggled together within her;*
> *and she said, 'If it is to be this way, why do I live?'*
> *So she went to inquire of the Lord."*
> —Genesis 25:22

God's answer to Rebekah's question may not have provided much comfort. He told her she was carrying twins who were nations (in other words, fathers of nations), and they would not get along well.

> *"And the Lord said to her, 'Two nations are in your womb, and two peoples, born of you shall be divided; the one shall be stronger than the other, the elder shall serve the younger.'"*
> —Genesis 25:23

In this chapter, we will explore the complex and tumultuous relationship between Jacob and Esau, twin brothers born to Isaac. Despite being destined for greatness, their lives took a dark turn as they became enemies, with deceit and revenge tearing them apart. Through Jacob's transformation and eventual reconciliation with his family, we can learn valuable lessons about faith, humility, forgiveness, and redemption. This chapter will focus on the journey of Jacob and the profound insights we can gain from his experiences, highlighting the power of faith, perseverance, and the ability to mend broken relationships.

The two sons of Isaac and Rebekah were physically different at birth, and they grew to be two very different young men. Firstborn Esau was bigger, stronger, and curiously described in verse 25 as coming out *"red, all his body like a hairy mantle."* Esau became a skillful and avid hunter. He was an outdoorsman, a more typically masculine individual.

Jacob, who entered the world after his brother, but clutched Esau's heel as he was delivered from Rebekah's womb, is described in verse 27 as a quiet man who lived in tents. In verse 29, we read that Jacob was at home cooking a stew. He was a softer individual, and although mere seconds separated their births, he was the younger brother, not the firstborn. Being the baby of the family, Jacob was closer to Rebekah and did not do all of the independent and mature things that Esau was doing as they were growing up. Jacob was a homebody, whereas Esau was always out and about, hunting, exploring, or spending time away from home. The Bible tells us that because of the twins' differences, their parents had favorites.

> *"Isaac loved Esau, because he was fond of game;*
> *but Rebekah loved Jacob."*
> —Genesis 25:28

It was certainly clear that Isaac favored Esau and Rebekah favored Jacob. It is likely that Jacob spent most or all of his time at home, either cooking or doing activities completely different from Esau's. His status did not help Jacob in terms of getting the firstborn blessing, though. In the Old Testament, the firstborn son would not only take over his father's role as head of the family, but would also receive a double share of the inheritance from him. Esau was the firstborn son, but Jacob was the golden child according to Rebekah.

Given how well Rebekah thought of Jacob, it is surprising to read about his attempt to buy Esau's birthright. In Genesis 25:29–34, we read that Jacob took advantage of Esau's hunger by agreeing to feed him on the proviso that Esau sell Jacob his birthright. For a bowl of soup, Esau gave up his right to the family property and the honor of leading the family. For a bowl of soup! Just because he was hungry. In a stunning example of immediate gratification trumping delayed gratification, Esau puts his simple need for food ahead of the great wealth and honor coming to him as the firstborn son of Isaac. On the surface this seems like a ridiculous trade, and the Bible notes this with a definitive closing statement in verse 34: *"Thus Esau despised his birthright."* It is essential to consider Jacob's state of mind when evaluating his actions. Jacob took advantage of Esau's vulnerability, exploiting his weakness to seize a significant birthright for a meager bowl of soup. Despite being aware of Esau's diminished capacity for rational decision-making, Jacob proceeded with his plan, demonstrating a lack of empathy and respect. This pattern of deception continued later in Jacob's life when he employed similar tactics against Laban, his future father-in-law. While Laban may have had his own questionable actions, it is still important to acknowledge that Esau did not deserve the level of deceit Jacob inflicted upon him.

It's a safe bet that Jacob told his mother that Esau had sold him his birthright, so Rebekah's plan to get Isaac's deathbed blessing for her favored son, rather than Esau, seems to be an attempt to make certain that Jacob would obtain the full rights of the firstborn. There were no witnesses to the plate-of-food deal between Jacob and Esau. As Jacob was Rebekah's favorite, she wanted to ensure that Jacob would get the blessings of birthright. Rebekah's duplicitous behavior would ultimately play in Jacob's favor. After all, even if Esau admitted to selling his birthright so cheaply, what good to Jacob was the birthright without the blessing?

Genesis 27 recounts a wicked deception perpetrated against Isaac. Ill, blind, and lying on his deathbed, Isaac requested that Esau go hunting and bring him a meal so that he could bless him.

> *"Then prepare for me savory food, such as I like, and bring it to me to eat, so that I may bless you before I die."*
> —GENESIS 27:4

Rebekah overheard this conversation and told Jacob to go to the flock and get her two choice young goats so that she could prepare a meal for Isaac. Jacob agreed with the plan but warned Rebekah of the risk that Isaac would be able to identify him by touch. It would all come undone if Isaac touched Jacob because, as Jacob said in Genesis 27:11, *"My brother Esau is a hairy man, and I am a man of smooth skin."*

After killing and cooking the flesh of the young goats, Rebekah used their skin to cover her favorite son's arms and hands so as to trick Isaac into believing that it was Esau who had come to receive his blessing. Remarkably, this somewhat elaborate scheme was successful, and Jacob added Isaac's blessing to the birthright he had "bought" from his brother. Esau arrived later to present food to his father and receive the blessing, but it was gone. He was too late. Apparently fully aware of the significance of the blessing and naturally desirous of it, Esau pleaded with his father for another blessing, but Isaac delivered a shattering refusal.

> *"Isaac answered Esau, 'I have already made him your lord, and I have given him all his brothers as servants, and with grain and wine I have sustained him. What then can I do for you, my son?'"*
> —Genesis 27:37

Esau was fighting mad, as you would expect, and threatened to kill Jacob. Genesis 27:41 records, in very unambiguous terms, how Esau felt as a result of being cheated out of his birthright and blessing. *"Now Esau hated Jacob…"* Rebekah learned that Esau was consoling himself with thoughts of murdering Jacob, so she sent her favorite son away to go and live with his uncle, Laban. She told Isaac, who backed her up by calling Jacob to his side, blessing him, and ordering him not to marry a Canaanite woman but to go to Paddan-aram and find a wife among Rebekah's kinsmen.

We aren't privy to Jacob's feelings about being sent far away from his home, but it is reasonable to assume they would have been mixed. On the one hand, he was being saved from his brother's wrath; on the other, this quiet homebody was being forced to leave the safety and security of home. Either way, this was going to be one of the most challenging times of his life. Where he once had the everyday familiarity of his life, now, for the first time, he must deal with the uncertainty of surviving on his own in a foreign land. During his journey traveling alone, his fear, sadness, frustration, feelings of isolation, and ideas of cowardice all must have overwhelmed him at times. I often wonder how many times he wanted to turn around and apologize to his brother. Or how many times he wanted to go running back to Rebekah and Isaac to ask for forgiveness. Instead, his fear of death kept him moving forward.

There are many times when we want to run and hide from our mistakes. We don't want to face our problems because the consequences are or may be greater than what we believe we are able to handle. As Jacob ran from Esau after tricking Isaac into giving him Esau's blessing, he knew he was a marked man. Rather than face Esau, Jacob chose to run and hide. I'm sure that as Jacob was running away, he was just trying to survive and figure out a plan. What good were the blessing and all of the riches when he could not cash in on them since he was running from Esau and from his whole family? He had gained the whole world, but at what cost? Had he forfeited his soul?

God was not done with Jacob in preparing him for the work that lie ahead. Jacob had to get life experience; he had hard lessons to learn.

After the acrimonious split in the family, the biblical narrative switches to a greater focus on Jacob. In Genesis 28:6–9, we read that when Esau heard what Isaac had told Jacob, he married a Canaanite woman purely out of spite. This was another thoughtless act, based purely on his emotions. Esau didn't usually give proper consideration to his choices, nor did his decisions carry any conviction. Instead of asking God for guidance, he just made up his mind and then dealt with whatever consequences followed.

Meanwhile, Jacob had a dream in which God visited him to renew the Abrahamic "father of many nations" promise.

> *"And he dreamed that there was a ladder set up on the earth, the top of it reaching to heaven; and the angels of God were ascending and descending on it. And the Lord stood beside him and said, 'I am the Lord, the God of Abraham your father and the God of Isaac; the land on which you lie I will give to you and to your offspring.'"*
> —Genesis 28:12–13

Jacob responded with worship, setting a pillar and anointing it with oil before calling that place Bethel, which means "the House of God." This happened in the aftermath of Jacob's selfish and deceptive behavior, which led to his estrangement from Esau and his banishment from his family. Yet, God came to him and spoke words of life to him at Bethel. Imagine the disappointment he must have had in himself; however, he needed to be reminded that God was still in control. Jacob needed encouragement in his time of sorrow, and God delivered. The conflict and resolution in Jacob's life all happened at once. God promised to keep him safe and someday return him back to his father.

As Jacob continued his journey, he finally came to a land where he met people near a well (Genesis 29:1:3). Jacob asked the men where they were from and found out that they knew his mother's family. While he was talking to them, a woman came to the well. In that moment Jacob was struck by something all too familiar. Something about the woman comforted Jacob and brought him peace. His reaction to the woman was very strong and emotional and must have shocked the men who looked on.

> *"Now when Jacob saw Rachel, the daughter of his mother's brother Laban, and the sheep of his mother's brother Laban, Jacob went up and rolled the stone from the well's mouth, and watered the flock of his mother's brother Laban. Then Jacob kissed Rachel, and wept aloud."*
> —Genesis 29:10–11

His actions seem over the top unless you consider the trauma he had been through. Jacob saw familiarity in the woman at the well; he saw his mother, Rebekah. Rachel was Rebekah's niece, so the physical resemblance was not surprising, but it was more than that. Jacob was close to his mother, and he missed her. After running away from the only family he had known and God speaking to him in his dream, that moment at the well—seeing Rachel and being so strongly reminded of his mother—may have been the first time the world seemed somewhat normal to him. Seeing Rachel certainly broke his heart, in a good way.

When he laid his eyes on Rachel, he immediately fell in love. Whether it was a form of trauma bonding from Jacob's perspective, or a sense of being rescued by Rachel, Jacob exploded with mixed emotions. When he kissed Rachel, he lifted up his voice and wept (Genesis 29:11). This may seem like an odd thing to do after kissing the love of your life. But not for Jacob. He was finally able to release the storm of emotions he had been carrying since being sent away from his home. Once he embraced her, Jacob must have decided that Rachel would be the woman he would marry.

It should also be noted that Jacob introduced himself after he kissed Rachel. So, in some ways, Rachel must have also felt some level of comfort or familiarity with him. Otherwise, why would she have so readily accepted a kiss from a stranger? We can assume it was mutual and the connection was felt by both sides. If Rachel hadn't felt the connection, she most likely would have made Jacob feel her true physical prowess. Considering Rachel was tending to the flock, she would have been a strong, independent woman, able to protect herself. Without consent, Jacob's attempt to kiss her may have resulted in a physical injury to him.

Although Jacob met and fell in love with Rachel, he then had to work for her father, Laban, for seven years in order to get Laban's permission to marry her. Naturally, he worked diligently for his prize, but the seven years seemed to him like only a few days because of how much he loved her (Genesis 29:20). Jacob's assiduous labor resulted in increased prosperity for Laban, who at some point realized he would lose his golden goose once the terms of the deal were fulfilled. In a "reap what you sow" moment, Laban deceived Jacob by sending his other daughter, Leah, into the marital tent for consummation. Laban justified his action by saying that Leah was the firstborn daughter and it was only right for her to marry before her younger sister. To soften the blow, Laban cut another deal with Jacob. A further seven years of labor would finally secure his beloved Rachel as his wife.

Imagine how Jacob must have felt about the way Laban treated him. Fourteen years to have the woman he wanted as his wife, with Laban continually moving the goalposts.

Oftentimes we work diligently at a job or on a business, but it feels like we are not getting anywhere. Frustration upon frustration, as we see no reward for our hard work. Dreams unfulfilled. During all that seemingly fruitless effort, we are slowly being molded, getting experience to prepare us for the more difficult jobs or times ahead. It's all about preparation and character development.

Thomas Edison said about his development of the light bulb, "*I did not fail. I found out 10,000 ways that it will not work.*" Just because we don't pass a test, or don't get the promotion right away, does not mean that those accomplishments will not happen. It just means that every time we may not accomplish the task at hand, we should look to God for guidance and patience. Then we will succeed. The key is obedience. If you are sure you are doing what God wants you to do, in the way God wants you to do it, then you can be doubly certain that God will honor that.

In another echo of the past, animosity rises between the sisters Leah and Rachel. Rachel, unable to bear children for Jacob, hands her maid Bilhah over for the job. Then Leah follows suit with her maid Zilpah. Rachel, Jacob's favorite, his true love if you like, remains barren while ten sons are born to her husband. Finally, in Genesis 30:22, "*God remembered Rachel, and God heeded her and opened her womb.*"

Jacob wished to return to his home country, but Laban, fearful of his fortunes nosediving without the all-encompassing favor of God that rested on Jacob, refused to let him go. So Laban made Jacob what was meant to be a bad bargain: Jacob would receive the spotted and speckled lambs and kids in the flock. In response, Jacob showed the same intelligence he used as a youth when he bested his brother, but now in a more mature form, as he used what he had learned of animal husbandry after years of work in the fields to best Laban's bad-faith offer of animals. It didn't hurt that God had given instructions to Jacob in his dreams—God, too, was confirming that it was time for Jacob to return home.

With God confirming that now was the time to leave (Genesis 31:3) and with the agreement of his wives (verse 16), Jacob finally left Paddam-aram and went home.

The only dark cloud on the horizon was that Esau was looking for him, presumably still intent on bloody revenge. To deal with the threat, Jacob sent messengers ahead to offer peace. In a miscommunication of potentially disastrous significance, the messengers reported back that Esau was on his way to meet Jacob with four hundred men. Jacob was afraid, but he didn't need to be. He prayed and sent presents to Esau in an effort to appease him. After Jacob had sent all of what he owned, he was left with just his immediate family. Jacob separated himself from his wives and eleven sons, leaving them to cross back over the Jabbok River, where he found himself all alone. It was there Jacob had his "wrestling" with God dream.

> *"Jacob was left alone; and a man wrestled with him until daybreak. When the man saw that he did not prevail against Jacob, he struck him on the hip socket; and Jacob's hip was put out of joint as he wrestled with him.*
> *Then he said, 'Let me go, for the day is breaking.'*
> *But Jacob said, 'I will not let you go, unless you bless me.'*

> *So he said to him, 'What is your name?' And he said, 'Jacob.'*
> *Then the man said, 'You shall no longer be called Jacob,*
> *but Israel, for you have striven with God and*
> *with humans, and have prevailed.'"*
>
> —Genesis 32:24–28

Before we completely dissect this story of Jacob wrestling with God, let us consider a few variables. First, let's consider Esau's life since Jacob departed his homeland. They had not seen each other for twenty years. The last time Jacob saw Esau, his brother was still in his prime: strong, healthy, and confident in his abilities. He was a proud and vital hunter. However, when Jacob stole his blessing and birthright, he became overwhelmed with hate and bitterness toward Jacob and his parents. Esau was so unhappy that he married a Canaanite just to spite his father. He would have gone through phases of self-doubt, not feeling loved by his parents, and cursing his brother, whom he had wanted to kill but could not find. Esau most likely stopped doing the things that made him happy as a result of his emotional state. His obsession became all-consuming, and the bitterness that had festered in his heart for so many years probably drained him physically. He might not have been the dominating, intimidating individual he once was when he and Jacob lived together.

On the other hand, Jacob had been doing manual labor for over twenty years. He had learned the craft of animal husbandry, the value of a good work ethic, negotiating for what he believed in, and perhaps most importantly, patience. With a lot of help from God, Jacob completely transformed his life. He was bigger, faster, and stronger as a result of the physical labor and his continuous desire for self-actualization. He too was a changed man by the time he was reunited with his brother. It is likely both men were, in fact, unrecognizable to each other when they met.

We return now to Jacob's dream. Jacob had been advised by his messengers that Esau was not happy and nothing seemed to be appeasing him. Despite Jacob's gifts, Esau continued to advance with over four hundred armed men. Any one of the messengers could have delivered a message of hope or potentially peace if Esau had truly wanted to send that message. The situation may have seemed hopeless, and Jacob was afraid for himself and his family, so he took precautions. He divided his camp in two, separating some of his riches and some of his people; then he waited. This is an indication of growth. Jacob was finally putting others' needs ahead of his own.

The story of Jacob wrestling with God until morning, as recorded in Genesis 32:22–32, is well known. Was Jacob having a bad dream or nightmare? Was he really wrestling God? Or could it have been Jesus incarnate, or was it Esau? If we examine the incident starting from verse 24, we can see the word "man" is in lowercase.

> *"Jacob was left alone; and a man wrestled with him until daybreak."*
> —Genesis 32:24

In the verses that follow, Jacob is said to be wrestling with a man, not with God. They also state that the man was pleading to be let go due to the beginning of daylight. Why would God be afraid of daylight? During the fight, the men continue to exchange words. Jacob refused to let the man go until the man blessed him. The man asked for Jacob's name, and he answered. Again, if it was God or even someone known to Jacob, why would he have asked for his name? When the man learned Jacob's name, he decided it was no longer appropriate.

> *"Then the man said, 'You shall no longer be called Jacob, but Israel, for you have striven with God and with humans, and have prevailed.'"*
> —GENESIS 32:28

The man then blessed Jacob, but not until he touched Jacob's hip, causing an injury.

A possible alternative to the widely accepted view that Jacob wrestled God is that Jacob was wrestling with Esau, and the latter was caught off guard by Jacob's newfound strength, size, and confidence. The man wanted the fight to be over before sunlight so that Jacob could not learn the true identity of the "man." If Esau was the "man," he wanted to get away to save face. When Jacob asked to be blessed, this time Esau recognized that Jacob had earned the blessing. Whatever Esau had been told by the messengers while he was pursuing Jacob, Esau was able to confirm all of the information for himself.

Now Jacob had truly struggled with God and man due to his conflicts with Laban's trickery involving Rachel and Leah. That is why Esau changed his name to Israel. Also, one final point about this specific incident is that in previous chapters, when God Himself changed a person's name, it became a permanent name change. For example, Abram was changed to Abraham and Sarai to Sarah. They were never again referred to by their old names. In Jacob's case, future references to him alternate between Jacob and Israel. In other words, both names were used after that renaming event.

When the lessons of Jacob's wrestling with God are taught, they are often taught from the perspective that Jacob wrestled with God in the physical sense or in the internal struggle of overcoming his deceptive nature. More often than not, it is easier for individuals to believe that Jacob wrestled with God or an angel. However, the alternate explanation I've put forward is plausible based on what we have learned about Jacob's and Esau's behaviors, physical transformations, and even their emotional states.

Jacob himself appears to strongly contradict this viewpoint.

> *"So Jacob called the place Peniel, saying,*
> *'For I have seen God face to face, and*
> *yet my life is preserved.'"*
> —Genesis 32:30

Whoever it was that he wrestled on that fateful night, Jacob's name was changed, and he was left with a permanent limp, a lasting physical sign of his encounter. The name change to Israel marks a change in his life. A rebirth of sorts. Jacob would no longer be the "trickster" or "deceiver" but would instead be a man who would follow God unconditionally. Several individuals in the Bible were given a name change. However, this particular one is monumental. Jacob received the name that would be used for God's people, who would thereafter be referred to as the Israelites. Jacob, now called Israel—which means "one who strives with God"—with all of his flaws, was still loved and chosen to do God's will. Up to this point in Jacob's life, he had deceived, lied, cheated, and been scared to confront all of his own mistakes and flaws. However, God still used Jacob and blessed him.

Maybe we need to stop fighting God's will and trying to wrestle with him just to get our way. Jacob was permanently injured by that encounter, but we should recognize that physical injury as a metaphor for our relationship with God. Physical or emotional scars are often viewed as a battle lost; rather, they should be seen—even welcomed—as a reminder of the battle fought and survived. If we can learn to accept His will and allow God back in our lives, all of those difficult times may not feel so purposeless.

With the dawn of a new day, and still fearful of Esau, Israel humbled himself, walking in front of his whole family, bowing seven times as the two parties approached one another (Genesis 33:3). Time and the Holy Spirit had done their work on Esau. In a beautiful and moving reunion, the older brother—the firstborn robbed of his birthright and blessing—ran to Israel and embraced him, and together they wept (Genesis 33:4).

Chapter 9

JOSEPH

PURPOSE IN THE PAIN

We have all experienced difficulty at times in our family relationships. No family is perfect, and Jacob's family was no exception. Joseph came from a family with many problems, but God still used him and his experiences. Joseph was not a perfect man; he had tremendous highs and appalling lows, some of which were his own fault while others were not.

In hard times, we often ask why God doesn't just make life easy. Why doesn't He protect us from all trouble? Because He could do that. The truth is, if we didn't have problems or challenges in life, if we didn't suffer, we would not need God, and we wouldn't reap the benefits of the refining process to mature into the best versions of ourselves ready to serve God. There is always purpose in pain, even when we can't see it or understand it.

Joseph was Jacob's eleventh son but the firstborn of his union with Rachel, who had been strangely barren for many years. Jacob loved Joseph more than his other children because Joseph was born when

Jacob and Rachel were much older. I believe Jacob also loved Joseph more than his other children because the wife he truly loved, Rachel, had given him a son that both of them had prayed for. Jacob and Rachel favored Joseph from the time of his birth. In a way, Joseph was able to reignite the type of love and passion Jacob must have felt when he first laid his eyes on Rachel and fell for her. Remember his exuberant display of emotion at the well—that initial shock of finding the person of his dreams? (Genesis 29:11) In that moment he fell in love with Rachel, who finally gave him a purpose to exist. Joseph, in a way, represented all of those qualities.

Joseph's brothers were often jealous of him and perhaps ganged up on him, but to be honest, Joseph did himself no favors by lording his "favorite" status over his brothers, and by being insensitive and conceited. He was also a snitch who brought bad reports about his brothers to his father. Only one such incident is recorded in the Bible (Genesis 37:2), but no doubt there were other times. It is interesting to note that the Bible introduces Joseph to the reader when he is seventeen years old, and the first comment about him is negative.

In verse 3 of chapter 37, Jacob gives Joseph a long-sleeved coat of many colors, which does not help calm relations with his brothers, who become even more angry. The Bible says they *"hated him and could not speak peaceably to him"* (Genesis 37:4). In the days of Jacob and Joseph, the majority of coats were possibly only one color and drab looking. A rich-colored coat made of some of the finest materials available was a garment most closely associated with royalty. Furthermore, it wasn't the kind of coat that the average person, or one who was doing manual labor, would be wearing. His brothers worked hard, farming or caring for the flocks. Joseph, dressed in his special coat, was not doing any physical labor, nor was he even dressed for it. We can well imagine the growing resentment felt by Joseph's brothers as they watched him prance around in his fancy coat, not lifting a finger to help.

Joseph's adolescence was marked by very typical teenage self-centeredness. Unfortunately, his favored status allowed the development of a sense of entitlement, and he had the mouth to go with it. It is not unusual for teens to speak without considering the impact of their words on others or taking into account the possible consequences. As they find their voices, many lack the maturity to be careful with their words.

Given Joseph's greatness in the kingdom of God and his powerful story, which is very well known, it is amazing to read what a lazy and arrogant brat he must have been. Oftentimes the youth of any generation are likewise spoken of as "lazy and arrogant." Think back to your youthful days. Did the older generation describe you in the same fashion?

Joseph started having dreams early on and, in yet another display of insensitivity, he shared them with his brothers.

> *"Once Joseph had a dream, and when he told it to his brothers, they hated him even more. He said to them, 'Listen to this dream that I dreamed. There we were, binding sheaves in the field. Suddenly my sheaf rose and stood upright; then your sheaves gathered around it, and bowed down to my sheaf.' His brothers said to him, 'Are you indeed to reign over us? Are you indeed to have dominion over us?' So they hated him even more because of his dreams and his words."*
>
> —Genesis 37:5–8

Joseph had another dream in which the sun, moon, and eleven stars were bowing down to him. In this second dream, the sun represented Israel/Jacob, the moon represented Rachel, and the eleven stars represented Joseph's eleven brothers. These dreams, of course, brought about more anger and jealousy from his brothers. Jacob rebuked Joseph, but I suspect not for having the dreams. Although displeased with his beloved son's lack of discretion, Jacob considered the dreams important (Genesis 37:11).

How did Joseph think his family would react to being told they would all bow down to him? He was asking for trouble, and trouble he duly received. Although it may appear that Joseph lacked empathy at this point, he was more likely just sharing his true feelings without considering the impact of his words. The consequences of his lack of sensitivity were to be more severe than he could have possibly imagined.

One day, Jacob sent Joseph to find his brothers, who were out feeding the flock. Joseph traveled from Hebron to Shechem and on to Dothan—a journey of roughly sixty-five miles. It is interesting to note that Joseph did not go with his brothers in the first place. Joseph either chose to stay home or his brothers did not want their lazy, big-mouth little brother to go with them. It would have been a relief for them to get away from him. The time Joseph's brothers spent away from him, and from their parents, certainly would have allowed for many conversations between them, but absence, in this case, did not make their hearts grow fonder.

> *"They saw him from a distance, and before he came near to them, they conspired to kill him. They said to one another, 'Here comes this dreamer. Come now, let us kill him*

> *and throw him into one of the pits; then we shall say that a wild animal has devoured him, and we shall see what will become of his dreams.'"*
> —Genesis 37:18–20

When Joseph finally reached his brothers, they immediately stripped him of his coat of many colors and threw him into a pit. Genesis 37:25 says the brothers then sat down to eat. They discussed what to do with Joseph, eventually agreeing to sell him to passing Midianite traders, which they did for twenty pieces of silver. At the time, that was the going rate for a slave.

Together the brothers then fabricated a story about Joseph being torn to pieces by a wild animal. They even ripped his coat, dipped it in goat's blood, and presented it to Jacob as proof that his beloved son was dead. While Jacob mourned his son, the very much alive Joseph was transported through the desert from Dothan into Egypt, where he was eventually sold to Pharoah's Captain of the Guard.

The journey would have been between 260 and 300 miles, and for a seventeen-year-old boy who was just sold into slavery by his own family, it would have been both physically and emotionally overwhelming. He must have felt angry, embarrassed, ashamed, and betrayed. Most likely he questioned every decision he had made up to that point. Did he regret bringing those bad reports about his brothers to his father? Lording his status over them? Sharing his dreams with them?

What happened to Joseph seems very harsh and unfair. After all, he had done no physical harm to any of his brothers, yet some of them wanted to kill him. And although they ultimately spared his life, or to be more accurate, "washed their hands" of the Joseph problem, the brothers brought unnecessary grief and pain to Jacob and Rachel as well as sentenced their little brother to a life in chains, exiled from his family. Whether we, the readers, are invited to feel sympathetic or not, Joseph's punishment was excessive and cruel, but not entirely unjustified. Often, when we hear about Joseph and his resilience during his ministry, the lessons taught are based on the premise that Joseph was completely innocent and the transgression against him was unreasonable, even if it was necessary. How quickly we forget that Joseph was a human being, a relatively normal teenager: arrogant, desperately lacking in empathy, and one who boasted to his brothers about his higher status. In fact, he rubbed it in their faces.

Despite what had happened, and irrespective of what conversations Joseph might or might not have had with God during his transport to Egypt regarding the degree of his own responsibility, we see God's grace at work.

> *"The Lord was with Joseph, and he became a successful man; he was in the house of his Egyptian master. His master saw that the Lord was with him, and that the Lord caused all that he did to prosper in his hands. So Joseph found favor in his sight and attended him; he made him overseer of his house and put him in charge of all that he had."*
> —Genesis 39:2–4

Read that verse again. Not only did God bless Joseph, but the blessing was so obvious that it caught the attention of his master. Youthful and previously foolish, Joseph clearly had a transformative experience on the road to Egypt—his own personal wilderness in which he sought to make sense of his life and make peace with God.

Joseph's enslavement quickly transformed into a career, as his recently discovered work ethic, together with the prosperity it brought to Potiphar's house, impressed the Captain sufficiently for Joseph to be made overseer of his master's home and possessions. Verse 6 tells us that Potiphar left all he had in Joseph's charge, completely trusting the young man. Potiphar no longer had anything to worry about. What a turnaround for Joseph! Potiphar must have seen Joseph's potential and intelligence when he bought him off the slave traders.

During his time as overseer of Potiphar's house, Joseph received some of the best education of his life in mathematics, organizational skills, relationship development, and communication skills, including how to negotiate positive outcomes for all aspects of Potiphar's home and business affairs. However, the most important skill Joseph learned was empathy.

What we see here is a type of rebirth for him, which was much needed. Joseph had been transformed by his suffering—refined by fire—and the new man was experiencing a life of blessing he would never have imagined when he was lying at the bottom of that pit, wondering if he would ever get out. The change in Joseph's fortune seems almost too good to be true. Something, we feel as a reader, must surely go wrong. And go wrong, it did.

The Bible describes Joseph as handsome and good-looking. Not just handsome or good-looking, but handsome *and* good-looking—so attractive to the eye, in fact, that Potiphar's wife took a liking to him. As we read in Genesis 39:7–12, Potiphar's wife tried to seduce Joseph in multiple ways and multiple times, over the course of several days at least, maybe even weeks. In that time, considering Joseph knew what to expect from Potiphar's wife, it would only make sense that he may have even put on additional clothing as protection.

Potiphar was not a fool, and he had also taken into account Joseph's appearance when he bought him. So it is possible that Joseph did not dress or appear the same way as the other slaves. After all, Joseph was a direct representation of Potiphar's house. So he may have been given additional clothing. In Genesis 39:12, you can read about the invitation that was to turn Joseph's life upside down once more. Potiphar's wife asked Joseph to have sex with her. He refused, providing a very good justification to the temptress for his refusal, but she was not easily deterred, and persisted with her attempted seduction of the young man. However, Joseph clearly told Potiphar's wife his decision, and his entire statement was based on his moral values and the impact the decision would have on Potiphar's house. This is what having a strong, empathetic side looks like. Joseph was considering someone else's perspective rather than his own.

Despite Joseph's strong stand, another major shift in his life was about to happen, much like when his brothers tore his coat and threw him into the pit.

> *"One day, however, when he went into the house*
> *to do his work, and while no one else was in the house,*
> *she caught hold of his garment, saying, 'Lie with me!'*
> *But he left his garment in her hand, and fled and ran outside.*
> *When she saw that he had left his garment in her hand,*
> *and had fled outside, she called out to the members of her*
> *household and said to them, 'See, my husband has brought*

> *among us a Hebrew to insult us! He came in to me to lie with me, and I cried out with a loud voice; and when he heard me raise my voice and cry out, he left his garment beside me, and fled outside."*
>
> —Genesis 39:11–15

As we read in verse 13, Joseph's garment was torn off of him by Potiphar's wife as Joseph was running away. She called on the men of the house and accused Joseph of trying to rape her. Joseph's reward for doing the right thing by not betraying his boss or offending God was to be thrown into prison. Potiphar very easily could have had Joseph put to death for such an act. However, Potiphar's decision indicates that perhaps he did not completely trust his wife. Also of note is that Potiphar was able to find Joseph so easily. After being accused of rape, Joseph could have run away to escape the consequences, but he chose to stay and stand on his innocence. Just like Joseph was stripped of his coat of many colors by his brothers and thrown into a pit, he was stripped of another garment by Potiphar's wife and thrown into another pit, this time a prison.

Both transformations in Joseph's identity came when life was quite easy for him, with very little trouble. You could say he was blindsided on both occasions. While Joseph lived in Jacob's house, he had nothing to worry about. And now Joseph was living in Potiphar's house as a slave, but he clearly was not living like a slave. He had other people in the house working for him, and he managed the household. Life had once again become too easy, and it was time for another shift to take place so that Joseph could be prepared for a major role in what would happen in Egypt. The next stage of Joseph's life education came from a strange place, not known for its emphasis on education. He would continue to be refined in the prison system.

Although Joseph may have initially thought so, God did not abandon him.

> *"But the Lord was with Joseph and showed him steadfast love; he gave him favor in the sight of the chief jailer."*
> —GENESIS 39:21

Joseph's prison term turned into an opportunity for service and advancement again. Just as Potiphar had placed Joseph in charge of everything, so did the Chief Jailer. At this point, Joseph the dreamer became the interpreter of dreams. First, he accurately predicted the fate of the Chief Cupbearer and the Chief Baker, who were both incarcerated for the crime of offending Pharaoh. Despite assurances from the Chief Cupbearer that he would mention Joseph to Pharaoh when he was released, Joseph languished in prison for another two years. As Joseph was being molded and prepared for his life ahead, the emotional burden of being forgotten again by those whom he had helped must not have been an easy thing for him. The knowledge that he had to continue to place his faith in God, rather than man, was repeatedly reinforced by his experiences.

It's amazing to witness how quickly good deeds can be forgotten by those who are the recipients once they have moved on with their lives without ever giving credit where credit is due. At this point in Joseph's "ministry," it is interesting to ruminate on what Joseph's life would have been like had the Chief Cupbearer remembered him. If Joseph had been released, he would have been considered a free man, but would he have returned to his family? Would he have been ready for that? Would Joseph have moved to another land? Had any of the preceding actions occurred, it would have been even more difficult to locate Joseph two years later when he would be needed for his gift of interpreting dreams.

While Joseph was still locked up, Pharaoh had a dream that greatly troubled him. The Pharaoh sought interpretation from his gang of wise men and magicians, none of whom could tell him what his dream meant. And that's when the Chief Cupbearer suddenly remembered Joseph. We have no idea how Joseph coped during his long and false imprisonment, but it is more than reasonable to assume that because he was innocent, it was perhaps not as bad a time as it could have been. Not only did he not lose his faith, but Joseph seems to have grown stronger.

Joseph washed and changed his clothes before being presented to Pharaoh, who asked him to interpret the dream. After boldly reminding the King of Egypt that his gift was from God (Genesis 41:16) and that God, not Joseph, would give Pharoah a favorable answer, he listened to the recount and then immediately gave Pharaoh the interpretation. Pharoah shared the second dream, and Joseph interpreted that one straightaway as well, telling the king that the two dreams had the same meaning: famine was coming to the land of Egypt. Joseph, again with great confidence, advises Pharoah how to prepare for the coming crisis to lessen its impact (Genesis 41:33–36).

As we read in Genesis 41:14, when Joseph was brought out of prison to be presented to the Pharaoh, he was again given new clothes. This third transformation in Joseph's life started his new identity. Now he was ready to take on the role that God had meant for him, even though Joseph may not have completely known it at the time.

Throughout Joseph's life, he went through three separate transformations that created and developed new identities for him. Dramatic shifts came when he least expected them. When life was easy and almost trouble free, it seemed that he was not growing or learning the skills needed for what God had prepared for him—much like our lives when everything is going well and when life is smooth sailing. A sudden wild and crazy turn brings about a transformation not just in our circumstances, but also in our identity. We often forget that this is God working in our lives and preparing us for what is coming. In those moments, we are at our weakest in acknowledging God's good works in us. We usually adopt a victim mentality of "God, why is this happening to me?" or "Why is this happening to my family?" We will often blame others rather than look past all of our grievances to allow God to show us the purpose in our pain.

Each of Joseph's new identities was represented by the clothing he wore or clothing that was given to him. The coat of many colors represented pride and ownership from Jacob to his son, and Joseph embraced that identity, imposing himself on his family. That coat was ripped off him, he was thrown into a pit, and then he was sold as a slave. Potiphar bought Joseph, being aware of and considering his looks and youthful vitality. He gave Joseph a new set of clothes that again represented a type of pride and ownership of Joseph. Again, those garments were ripped off him, this time by Potiphar's wife, and Joseph was thrown into the pit of the prison system. Finally, when his time came to serve Pharoah, Joseph was cleaned, washed, and given a new set of clothes. And when Joseph spoke to Pharaoh, he gave glory to God and told the Pharaoh that God was the only one who could truly provide the meaning of his dreams.

This new identity freed Joseph from the debilitating weight of his past sins, mistakes, and choices. Joseph served the Pharaoh; however, he did it with complete faith and in a way that honored God. Joseph's pain and suffering ultimately prepared him for greatness by breaking the power of his past, releasing him from the consequences of familial choices that had been made by his father Jacob, his grandfather Isaac, and his great-grandfather Abraham. In becoming his own man, outside the limits of his family, Joseph broke the generational chains and followed his Redeemer into a life of service that glorified God.

> *"This proposal [Joseph's advice in the previous verses] pleased Pharaoh and all his servants. Pharaoh said to his servants, 'Can we find anyone else like this— one in whom is the Spirit of God?' So Pharaoh said to Joseph, 'Since God has shown you all this, there is no one so discerning and wise as you. You shall be over my house, and all my people shall order themselves as you command; only with regard to the throne will I be greater than you.'"*
> —GENESIS 41:37–40

As a result of trusting God and speaking without fear, Joseph found himself again, for a third time, in a senior management role. Only this time it was Pharaoh who placed Joseph in a position of authority. This promotion cannot be overstated. Joseph, at the relatively young age of thirty (you may recall that Jesus began his public ministry at the same age), became the second most powerful man in Egypt (Genesis 41:41–45).

Joseph made preparations for the coming famine and, having married Pharaoh's daughter, also found time to father two sons, Manasseh and Ephraim. When the famine hit, Jacob sent Joseph's brothers to Egypt because he'd heard there was grain to be bought there. The brothers were brought before Joseph, presumably because they were foreigners, and Joseph recognized them instantly. They, however, did not recognize him. Remember that approximately thirteen years had passed, and Joseph was dressed as an Egyptian, presumably with his face painted as nobles and royals did in those days.

How much had Joseph thought about his brothers and what they did to him over all the years he lived in Egypt? Clearly, he had not forgiven them because when they showed up to ask to buy grain, he *"treated them like strangers and spoke harshly to them"* (Genesis 42:7). Where is the grace? God had been so good to Joseph, yet when he saw his own flesh and blood begging for food, he accused them of being spies and had them thrown in jail. After three days, Joseph presented them with a way out. All but one of the brothers were free to leave. Simeon was chosen by Joseph himself as the brother to remain in prison. Joseph ordered the others not to return to Egypt without Benjamin, who had remained home on this first journey. Benjamin was Joseph's full brother, the youngest child of Jacob and Rachel.

The encounter was emotional torture for Joseph, who, at one point, had to leave so he could cry in private (Genesis 42:24). Despite his overwhelming emotion, he pulled himself together and repeated the deal he was offering. The brothers, in great anguish themselves, agreed, and Joseph provided them with provisions for their journey. Given Joseph's emotional state, we must question his motives for treating his brothers so severely and for not simply revealing himself to them and reconciling with them. God showed Joseph mercy, but he either could not or would not pass it on to his brothers. His behavior seems vindictive.

After initially refusing to allow Benjamin to travel to Egypt, Jacob relented, but the brothers did not leave until they had eaten everything they had and needed more. When Joseph saw the brothers coming and noted that Benjamin was with them, he ordered his stewards to prepare a feast and invite the brothers to dine with him. You can imagine how afraid they were, but the steward assured them they had nothing to fear. Once they were ready, they took gifts to meet Joseph, and when they saw him, they bowed down to him. Did Joseph remember his teenage dreams at that moment? He must have because the recounting of those dreams to his brothers had been a major contributor to the enmity between him and them.

Overcome a second time with emotion, Joseph left the room, going away to weep privately. You can imagine the outpouring of pent-up grief, the strength it took for him to continue to conceal his true identity from his brothers, the torrent of mixed feelings pounding inside his head. Joseph composed himself, washed his face, and returned to dine with them, providing a serving for Benjamin that was five times larger than the others were given. Still, Joseph kept his secret, and the following day, he took his revenge further by framing Benjamin for theft and having him arrested (Genesis 44:1–17).

At Joseph's house, Judah stepped forward to beg for Benjamin's life, falling once more at the feet of the brother he had sold into slavery. The same man he did not recognize as the victim of his jealousy stood before him with the power of life and death in his hands. Finally, after hearing Judah out, in particular how grief and anguish were killing his father, Joseph could stand no more. He shouted at everyone to leave the room except his brothers, and at last revealed himself to them. Picture the scene as loud wailing filled the room, heralding the reconciliation of Jacob's sons, one and all.

The brothers returned to Jacob to bring him the good news that Joseph was alive. There is no talk of recrimination, no request for explanation.

> *"But when they told him all the words of Joseph that he had said to them, and when he saw the wagons that Joseph had sent to carry him, the spirit of their father Jacob revived. Israel said, 'Enough! My son Joseph is still alive. I must go and see him before I die.'"*
> —GENESIS 45:27–28

Jacob was so overwhelmed with joy that Joseph was alive after so many years, his spirit revived. He silenced all talk and announced that he would travel to Egypt. It's interesting to note here that the Bible now refers to Jacob as Israel. Israel took the whole family to Egypt and settled them in Goshen, where he lived for seventeen years. After blessing his sons (Genesis 48 and 49), Jacob died at the age of 147.

Joseph enjoyed almost indescribable prosperity and was surrounded by family, yet he still apparently held a grudge against his brothers. It was not until after Jacob's death that Joseph finally forgave them. The brothers believed that may have been the case and seemed convinced that with their father out of the picture, Joseph may have sought some final terrible revenge on them.

> *"Realizing that their father was dead,*
> *Joseph's brothers said, 'What if Joseph still bears*
> *a grudge against us and pays us back in full*
> *for all the wrong that we did to him?'"*
> —Genesis 50:15

It is shocking to think that a man who enjoyed the favor of God for so long could have carried a root of bitterness all that time. Perhaps it was only what the brothers thought, because when they approached him to ask forgiveness, he granted it willingly. They bowed down to Joseph a second time, and he forgave them.

Joseph died at the age of 110 with the Israelites entrenched in Goshen, where they flourished until a new king, who did not know Joseph, came to the throne of Egypt and brought with him the beginning of a dark time in Israel's history.

Joseph may not have done anything drastically sinful or life-altering, yet he still needed to be prepared for what God had in store for him. God needed his people in Egypt, and that was Joseph's purpose. In those moments of despair, Joseph had no idea what was going on. There were perhaps times when he drifted away from God, in a comfortable and forgetful way, moving from where God wanted him to be. God orchestrated the rebirth and refining of Joseph because God always achieves what He wants to achieve. He had a plan, and He could not be thwarted. What we want out of life may not necessarily be what we need, and more often than not, what we need does not always equate to what happens. The key to navigating life's challenges is God's grace. Be thankful, be faithful, and remember that God, your Father, loves you and wants what's best for you.

On a final note, the three phases of Joseph's life can also be representative of what may happen in our own lives. A journey of purification. When Joseph was finally washed and cleaned, he was being prepared to be presented before the "King," much like our own profession of faith in Christ. Once an individual professes to follow Christ and is saved, it does not mean that life is going to get easier. Rather, it means that you've become a target of temptation and someone for Satan to chase. Like Joseph, we must learn to shed our old ways and be prepared to be presented before our King.

Chapter 10

MOSES

FRUSTRATED DISOBEDIENCE WITH GOD'S LOVE

In some form or fashion, we have all been disobedient to God. Unfortunately, it's in our nature to sin. God gave Moses many opportunities to adhere to the plan and follow it exactly as God had instructed.

Not being able to maintain a balance between emotionality and rationality can and will lead to decisions that will impact you and others in unimaginable ways. Consider what happens to us when our emotionality increases. Our basic decision-making and rationality decrease. The only way to bring our rational decision-making to a balanced state is to control our emotional state. This was Moses' struggle. Moses, being a human, could not escape the temptations of pride, arrogance, sadness, shame, frustration, and anger. At times, he had a difficult time controlling these emotions, which impacted his decision-making—and, in turn, distracted Moses from following God's plan. But through all of Moses' emotional highs and lows, God was always present. God had a hand in Moses' life from his birth to the moment he took his last breath.

Moses' story begins three hundred years after the death of Joseph and all his brothers. The entire generation has passed away. Jacob's descendants, who relocated to Egypt to join Joseph, had multiplied.

> *"But Israelites were fruitful and prolific;*
> *they multiplied and grew exceedingly strong,*
> *so that the land was filled with them."*
> —Exodus 1:7

A new king, although the title would later be changed to Pharoah, ruled Egypt and did not know Joseph (Exodus 1:8). With the passing of time also comes the passing of memories and alliances, but Joseph had left a huge legacy. Everyone in Egypt would have heard stories about him. Furthermore, the new king would have had some method of keeping historical records, and would certainly have known all the good Joseph did for Egypt. When the Bible says the king did not know Joseph, it means he disregarded Joseph's history of good deeds for political purposes. By diminishing Joseph's role in Egypt, the king was able to wipe the slate clean, thereby justifying his horrific deeds that would follow.

The king felt threatened by the sheer volume of Israelites who were becoming increasingly more prosperous than their Egyptian counterparts, and he would have been under pressure to do something about the problem. Racism is as old as time itself. Rather than seeing Egypt as one nation and one people with diverse backgrounds, embracing the kind of multiculturalism we take for granted now in the modern world, Pharaoh forced the Israelites into slavery and persecuted them.

> *"The Egyptians became ruthless in imposing tasks
> on the Israelites, and made their lives bitter with hard service
> in mortar and brick and in every kind of field labor.
> They were ruthless in all the tasks
> that they imposed on them."*
> —Exodus 1:13–14

Determined to reduce the Hebrew population, Pharaoh ordered certain midwives to kill the Hebrew boys as they were born. The midwives disobeyed Pharaoh's orders because they feared God. The Hebrew population continued to grow. When that failed, Pharoah issued a command to all his people, that all boys born to Israelite families should be thrown into the Nile and drowned. Life was miserable and dangerous for the Israelites in Goshen, living under the cruel and racist authority of the Pharaoh.

Moses was the child of an Israelite woman. When Moses was just three months old, she felt she could conceal her son no longer, so she put him into a papyrus basket and cast him out on the waters of the Nile. He was discovered by Pharaoh's daughter and, thereafter, raised in the Pharoah's home. He was adopted by Pharaoh's daughter and so received an upbringing and an education fit for a prince. Indeed, that is what he was. Moses, the child of a Hebrew slave, was a Prince of Egypt.

As Moses lived his "princely" life, I'm sure there were times he may have felt out of place, or perhaps not completely connected to his family due to a strange, and at that time inexplicable, feeling of being drawn to the Hebrew slaves. He must have retained some mysterious affinity with them, not knowing that he was one of them. Moses, already sympathetic to the plight of the Israelites, most likely witnessed numerous atrocities against them until finally he could not take it anymore. This is the first example, and one of many more to come, where Moses was not able to control his emotions.

> *"One day, after Moses had grown up,*
> *he went out to his people and saw their forced labor.*
> *He saw an Egyptian beating a Hebrew, one of his kinsfolk.*
> *He looked this way and that, and seeing no one he*
> *killed the Egyptian and hid him in the sand."*
> —Exodus 2:11–12

It is unclear from the biblical narrative whether Moses did that because, despite being an Egyptian prince, he still identified as Hebrew, or because he had a well-developed sense of justice, or both. In either case, the following day when he tried to intervene in a dispute between two Hebrews, they resented it and threatened to reveal that he had killed the slave driver. Soon after, when Moses learned that Pharoah knew what he had done and sought to kill him, he ran away, fleeing Egypt and the consequences of his crime.

What a dramatic fall from a life of privilege and power, to be flung into a life in exile. How difficult it must have been for Moses to be caught in the tension between Egypt and Israel. He belonged in two worlds and was ultimately unable to reconcile himself to that situation. His act of violence was surely not only a justifiable response to cruelty, but also an expression of his frustration. Despite the terror of being on Pharoah's death list, Moses may also have felt relieved to get out of Egypt. It may simply have become too much for him to handle.

Moses settled in the land of Midian (Exodus 2:15–21), where he married, had children, and spent forty years hiding out, working as a shepherd. While Moses built a new life for himself in Midian, the situation for the Israelites in Egypt worsened. The Pharaoh died, but his successor kept his sandaled Egyptian foot firmly on the throat of the Hebrews to such an extent that the oppressed Israelites could suffer it no longer, and they cried out to God.

> *"God heard their groaning, and God remembered his covenant with Abraham, Isaac, and Jacob."*
> —Exodus 2:24

The time had come for God's people, the chosen ones, to be delivered, and God selected an unlikely hero to lead their rescue. Moses, the former Prince of Egypt, a murderer, the man who hid in the desert for forty years, was looking after his father-in-law's flock beyond the wilderness when God spoke to him.

> *"There the angel of the Lord appeared to him in a flame of fire out of a bush; he looked, and the bush was blazing, yet it was not consumed. Then Moses said, 'I must turn aside and look at this great sight, and see why the bush is not burned up.' When the Lord saw that he had turned aside to see, God called to him out of the bush, 'Moses, Moses!' And he said, 'Here I am.'"*
> —Exodus 3:2–4

God then told Moses to remove his sandals and announced Himself as the God of Moses' father, the God of Abraham, the God of Isaac, and the God of Jacob (Exodus 3:6). Moses was afraid. Who wouldn't be? Moses hid his face as God revealed to him His plan to set His people free. In fact, He commissioned Moses to go to Egypt and confront Pharaoh (Exodus 3:10). One thing is for sure: Moses had no intention of ever returning to the land of the Pharaoh. Ever.

Yet God ordered him to go, dismissing his protests and excuses, and dealing with his objections with firmness and patience. Moses gave God several reasons why he would not be able to get the people out of Egypt. First, he said, "Who am I?" He was nobody. He had no authority. No army. No power. He explained that he could not go alone, but God told him he would not be alone (Exodus 3:12). Next, he told God that he needed a name. How could he go to his people and just say "the God of your ancestors" has sent me? They would need a name. So, God told Moses his name was YAHWEH, which is Hebrew for "*I AM THAT I AM*" (Exodus 3:14, KJV). Moses then suggested that the people of Israel may not believe what he says. What should he do then?

God did a couple of seemingly superficial magic tricks to convince Moses—the staff turning into a snake, and his hand becoming leprous then being healed—but Moses was still reluctant. In verse 10 of Chapter 4, he bemoaned his lack of eloquence. God assured him of his ability to overcome his natural shortcomings with divine assistance, but Moses pleaded with God to choose someone else to do the job.

The anger of the Lord was then kindled against Moses. (Exodus 4:14). We know God is slow to anger, so it is almost amusing to think about Moses' childish disobedience and questioning, and his arguing with God. God Almighty, the great I Am, called Moses to be His man on the ground, His agent of change, and He sweetened the offer by making several promises that He would supply everything Moses lacked to accomplish the mission. But Moses would not step up.

What was going on in his head? Fear. Shame. Lack of confidence. It could not have been a lack of belief because God was right there talking to him. Moses' emotional response—his instinctive fear reaction—held him back. Irrespective of the reason behind Moses' refusal, God agreed to send Moses' elder brother, Aaron, with him to Egypt. Aaron would do the talking, and with that final piece of help, Moses agreed to go and packed his family and his goods into a cart and headed to Egypt. God warned Moses that Pharaoh would make trouble and that releasing the Hebrews from slavery in Egypt would not be a straightforward matter.

God empowered Moses and Aaron to approach Pharoah and ask him to *"let my people go so that they may celebrate a festival to me in the wilderness"* (Exodus 5:1). Pharoah refused and, because he was angered by the demand, decided the Hebrews were lazy and forced them to make bricks without any straw, which made the work even harder.

Pharoah's continued recalcitrance resulted in a series of plagues on Egypt. Exodus 7:14 to Exodus 12:32 recounts the ten plagues that God visited on the Egyptians; the first nine were blood, frogs, lice, flies, the plague on the cattle, boils, hail, locusts, darkness. After each plague, Pharaoh would relent, agreeing to let the Hebrews go, only to almost immediately harden his heart and change his mind once more, which led to enduring another plague. The tenth and final one was the death of the firstborn, from which arose the Hebrew Passover festival. After experiencing the loss of his own firstborn, Pharaoh caved in to God's demand, and this time he appeared to mean it. Fearful, grief-stricken, and perhaps humbled, at least temporarily, he decided to set his Hebrew slaves free.

> *"Then he summoned Moses and Aaron in the night,*
> *and said, 'Rise up, go away from my people, both you and*
> *the Israelites! Go, worship the Lord, as you said.*
> *Take your flocks and your herds, as you said, and be gone.*
> *And bring a blessing on me too!'"*
>
> —Exodus 12:31–32

Four hundred and thirty years after Jacob's family settled in Goshen, Moses, with staff in hand, led approximately two million Jews out of Egypt and into the wilderness. It was to be a circular, wandering journey of forty years. A question often arises about why the Jews spent forty years wandering around in the desert when God had promised them a permanent home. The distance between Cairo and Jerusalem was approximately three hundred miles. Deuteronomy 1:2 suggests it would have taken approximately eleven days' journey from Horeb, via Mount Seir, to Kadesh-barnea. This refers to the pathway between Egypt and Israel that would have been traveled during Moses' time in the desert, around 1446 BC.

Why did the eleven-day journey take forty years? A possible reason is the need for generational change. The Jews who were adults or elderly were set in their ways and not as committed to God. So wandering in the desert was necessary for those nonbelievers to either pass on from this earth or become believers in God's almighty power. God's people were simply not ready to take possession of the Promised Land.

Following Moses' meeting with the Lord in the burning bush and the subsequent negotiation, Moses walked in obedience, carrying out every one of God's instructions to the letter. Despite the complaints of the people, who soon regretted their decision to leave Egypt, Moses remained faithful and steadfast, dealing with their grievances by seeking God and following His instructions. In that way, the Israelites had food to eat and water to drink. Moses, after some wise advice from Jethro, instituted a kind of government and an administrative system, then later met with God on Mount Sinai to receive the Ten Commandments. He resolutely interceded for the Israelites when they inexplicably rebelled against God and forced Aaron to construct a golden calf, which they then worshiped while Moses was on the mountain.

Unfortunately, continual complaints, rebellions, and various other problems persisted throughout the journey. Moses often had to pray that God would have mercy on His people and forgive them. As a result of these troubles, the wandering cycle continued, as God continued on with His plan, preparing His people to enter the Promised Land.

Eventually, the burden of leadership and the constant grumbling of the people wore Moses out and revealed his human weakness. Imagine for a moment the frustrations, hardships, and constant uncertainty of not knowing when your journey would end. Moses led the Jews for forty years, and during that time he must have faced some of the most difficult times of his life, being reminded daily of his failures by those he loved and cared for. How many times in our lives do we face scrutiny and vacillation by friends, family members, or coworkers? Imagine facing that for forty years! It's no wonder Moses cracked.

Moses also became accustomed to the Israelites' dependence on him. At times, it seemed they were following Moses more than God. That transactional relationship became part of Moses' identity and was difficult for him to shed.

Much like the Hebrews wandered aimlessly in the desert, Moses wandered away from the path of obedience. At times, his job was simply too much for him. Numbers 11:10–15 records one occasion—there were probably others—when he voiced his unhappiness, wondering aloud if God was punishing him. He then progressed from that complaint to a specific act of disobedience.

Before discussing what he did, we must also understand that Moses had already performed several miracles with God's guidance and instructions. In Exodus 17, the Israelites found themselves in a very difficult predicament. They were in the desert, but they had no water. The Israelites approached Moses and once again laid their hardships and complaints before him.

> *"The people quarreled with Moses, and said, 'Give us water to drink.' Moses said to them, 'Why do you quarrel with me? Why do you test the Lord?' But the people thirsted there for water; and the people complained against Moses and said, 'Why did you bring us out of Egypt, to kill us and our children and livestock with thirst?'"*
>
> —Exodus 17:2–3

Moses asked God for help, and God told him to gather the people and all the elders. God would stand on a particular rock; Moses was to strike that rock and the needs of the people would be met. Once the people were assembled, Moses struck the rock and water flowed freely from it, more than enough for everyone to drink.

The specific incident of disobedience happened in the Desert of Zin in a place called Meribah Kadesh (Numbers 20:2–13). Again, there was no water to drink, so the Israelites protested to Moses and Aaron, lamenting the exodus because they said that at least in Egypt they had water. Moses and Aaron prayed, and God instructed Moses to speak to a particular rock, to command it to bring forth water. Perhaps recalling the previous time, when he had struck a rock to provide water, Moses disobeyed God, and instead of speaking to the rock, he struck it twice with unnecessary force. In his anger, Moses referred to the Israelites as "rebels" and chastised them for their continual whining and murmuring. Imagine the look on Moses' face when he struck the rock the first time and no water flowed. Angry and probably embarrassed, Moses had to strike it a second time. Water flowed and the people drank, but God was displeased.

Moses essentially took credit for the water flowing from the rock instead of giving the credit to God. Moses seemed to bask in the glory of his success. The people began to worship or honor Moses instead of rightfully honoring and glorifying God. If Moses talked to the rock, commanding it to release water in Yahweh's name, as God had instructed him to do, and had he given glory to God instead of making it appear as though he was the one making the water appear from the rock, the Jews' faith in God may have grown. Instead, they began to shift their focus away from God, toward Moses.

When God specifically told him to talk to the rock, Moses did what he felt was necessary due to his emotional state and irrational mindset. Reacting in that way to the people's complaints and demands became his default response. In other words, he let his emotional side overrule the rational part of his brain. And it was there, in that moment of irrationality, that Moses made one of the biggest mistakes of his life. It must have felt good for him, albeit momentarily, to have the Israelites cheering and loving him as though he were a god. It also seems likely that in that specific moment the Israelites may have solidified Moses' place in their history books as one of their most important prophets.

However, God's plan of having the Israelites look past Moses and onto God became further diminished. Moses was to represent God, not be a god. Him striking the rock to release the water for the Hebrews may look like a relatively minor incident when compared with the other events of the Exodus, but that moment was clearly of great spiritual significance. It was God's chosen servant rejecting Him, taking glory for himself.

Throughout our lives, we find ourselves in similar situations, where one act of disobedience can lead to years and years of suffering. I recall a specific choice I made at work that impacted several individuals I was close to. My poor choice led to suffering directly felt by others. However, I too had to face the consequences of my poor decision, which led to several years of embarrassment and shame, and the loss of numerous close friends. There are still times when I look back and think, *How could I be so foolish? Why did I do that?* I can't go back and undo the decisions made. I can only live with the outcome, learn from those mistakes, and ensure that they don't happen again.

Some time after the striking-of-the-rock incident, Moses was told to go up the mountain, where God showed him the Promised Land. It was here God also delivered the bad news that because Moses was now numbered among the disobedient, he would not enter it. Aside from his faith and obedience through Israel's forty years in the wilderness, he would have been motivated by hope—the hope of leading God's people into the land of milk and honey. However, it was not to be, and in that moment he would have realized that he had only himself to blame. Despite his disappointment, Moses kept his eye on the bigger picture—the future of his people.

> *"Moses spoke to the Lord, saying, 'Let the Lord, the God of the spirits of all flesh, appoint someone over the congregation who shall go out before them and come in before them, who shall lead them out and bring them in, so that the congregation of the Lord may not be like sheep without a shepherd.' So the Lord said to Moses, 'Take Joshua son of Nun, a man in whom is the spirit, and lay your hand upon him…'"*
> —Numbers 27:15–18

In Deuteronomy, we read the speech Moses gave in the fortieth year of the Israelites' sojourn in the desert. He was 120 years old, and these were his parting words, his final oration and perhaps the longest speech ever recorded, in which he recounts the journey, goes through the law, and then commands the people to be obedient. The speech takes up the first thirty chapters of the book of Deuteronomy. When Moses finished speaking, he anointed Joshua, the son of Nun, an Ephraimite who had been by Moses' side throughout the journey in the wilderness, faithfully attending to him and the service of the tabernacle. Joshua and Caleb were the only ones among the twelve spies sent to Canaan to bring back a positive report. After anointing Joshua, Moses recounted the words of a song that we now call The Song of Moses (Deuteronomy 32). Finally, he pronounced a blessing over the people, naming all twelve tribes who bore the names of the sons of Jacob.

Once the formalities were concluded, Moses ascended Mount Nebo, where God showed him the Promised Land. Step back into that specific moment when Moses was standing atop Mount Nebo and once again talking to God. Moses knew that moment was different from all the other times he and God had interacted. God must have spoken to him in that peaceful, loving way as to say, "Moses, you have done a good job, and I know you're tired. You need to know something…" God showed Moses the entire land and valley, the land of milk and honey, and Moses looked at it in awe. The fact that a reference is made to Moses' health and vitality, and specifically his eyesight, leads me to believe that God may have given Moses a vision, allowing him to see into the future, to see his people living in the land and thriving. After showing Moses that great vision, it must have been so hard for God to tell Moses that he would not be able to enter the Promised Land. Moses must have been devastated, but at the same time, perhaps he sensed a supernatural peace. God Himself, the God of his fathers, was standing there next to him to deliver the message that he would not experience the fulfillment of the promise. He had done all the hard work, but he would not be there to see it through.

As a son may talk to his father after learning the consequences of his disobedience, would Moses have tried to justify his actions to God or to ask for one more chance? Just as a father feels the pain of having to discipline his child after a wrongdoing, God too must have felt sad for His son, knowing that Moses had truly worked hard and did a multitude of difficult tasks, suffering greatly throughout his life, especially in the stress of leading a nation of grumblers. As much as it must have pained God to see one of His children suffering in His presence, God also knew that He could not leave Moses in that moment of despair. It was time for him to come home and to finally get some much-needed rest. As Moses sat down with his back to a rock, his back to the Chosen Land, a land he would never be able to walk in, he took his last breath. God carried him off to bury him in an act of great compassion and unconditional love. Perhaps concerned with the possibility that the Israelites would treat Moses' burial place as a holy place, He buried him in secret. Only God knows where one of His chosen sons has his final resting place. It's a poetic and perfect ending to the life lived by Moses, who was truly carried by God.

It sometimes seems like we are doomed to be forever at the mercy of the negative consequences of our bad decisions, but God can redeem our mistakes. He is our redeemer.

However, you should know and trust that God will use your pain and suffering to lay a foundation in you so that you too can become a resilient and powerful individual. In your suffering, you may feel the depths of anguish, and begin to see all of your flaws. That's not a bad thing. Remember, God knows that we will never be perfect. We have our flaws and our scars from the times we've suffered. Just know that God can and will use your flaws to ensure you are still chosen for His plan. The pain we suffer, whether physical or emotional, will never be wasted; rather, it will lay a foundation for a better future. Just stay the course; God is faithful.

Chapter 11

SAMSON

IDLE MINDS CAN LEAD TO DARK TIMES

Joshua 24:31 tells us that Israel served the Lord all the days of Joshua and also all the days of the elders who outlived Joshua and had known all the work that the Lord did for Israel. However, after Joshua's death, the Israelites fell back into their evil and disobedient ways, and for over 500 years, God often allowed other nations to rule over them. This period of Israel's history, before God gave them their first king, is recorded in the Book of Judges. During these mostly dark days for Israel, God raised up individuals to lead His people. Among them were Israel's first female leader, the warrior prophet named Deborah, and Gideon, who is best remembered for his sheep fleece test.

Ruling families bickered and warred against each other, contributing to an overall decline in the well-being of the Israelites such that once again God needed a deliverer to free them. The various tribes inhabiting Canaan were collectively referred to as Philistines, and the ongoing enmity between them and the Israelites was not only over land, but also a clash of worldviews. After the death of Abdon, son of Hillel, things went downhill again.

> *"The Israelites again did what was evil in the sight of the Lord, and the Lord gave them into the hand of the Philistines forty years."*
> —JUDGES 13:1

During this time, Samson was born. Samson is unique among the leaders whom God raised up in that he famously had superhuman strength. Samson, whose name means "sunshine," was born sometime between 1045 BC and 1000 BC, during a dark period of Israel's history. Seven times the nation of Israel had turned from God, and when Samson was born, they found themselves again under the oppressive rule of the Philistines.

Although we may not have the strength of Samson, we can all see a small version of ourselves in different aspects of Samson's life. Whether it's his intellect, his strength, or the various dark emotions Samson felt and displayed, his story can teach us the lesson that once we can identify our God-given gifts, which we all have, we must also submit them to God to be used in a way that pleases and glorifies Him. It is easy to squander God-given talent on worldly pursuits, but we should ask God what good we can do with those gifts and abilities rather than surrendering them to our own desires or to the devil.

Following a familiar pattern, God selected parents who seemed desperate for a child. A man named Manoah, a Danite, had a barren wife. God's choice of certain individuals for significant tasks sometimes seems unfathomable, but those He calls, those He chooses, will rise to the occasion and overcome all difficulties. The story of Samson began with the announcement of his birth by the Angel of the Lord, making Samson one of the few people in scripture whose birth was divinely pre-announced to his parents:

> *"And the angel of the Lord appeared to the woman and said to her, 'Although you are barren, having borne no children, you shall conceive and bear a son. Now be careful not to drink wine or strong drink, or to eat anything unclean, for you shall conceive and bear a son. No razor is to come on his head, for the boy shall be a nazirite to God from birth. It is he who shall begin to deliver Israel from the hand of the Philistines.'"*
>
> —JUDGES 13:3–5

Samson's mother was instructed to abstain from consuming alcohol, eating unclean foods, and cutting her son's hair. As we'll learn a little later, Samson's strength was derived from his long hair, which symbolized his obedience to God.

Soon thereafter their son was born to them, and they named him Samson. He was brought up as a Nazirite according to the Angel's instructions; Nazarite means one who is separated or consecrated. Judges 13:24–25 tells us that God blessed Samson as he grew and, more importantly, *"the spirit of the Lord began to stir in him."*

As a young man, Samson traveled to Timnah, saw a woman he desired, then demanded his parents marry him to the woman. The problem was that the woman was a Philistine, and the law of Moses forbade marriage to foreigners. Israelites had to marry Israelites to avoid being culturally and spiritually contaminated. Samson's parents attempted to talk him out of the marriage, telling him it was wrong, but Samson stubbornly insisted, saying he did not care that she was a Philistine woman. We can imagine Samson's parents fretting over his obsession with the foreign woman, but as they were unable to resist him, they traveled to Timnah to find the woman so that Samson could marry her.

As Samson and his parents traveled to Timnah, Samson happened to find himself in a vineyard alone. Samson walked through the vineyard, and he came upon a lion.

> *"The spirit of the Lord rushed on him,*
> *and he tore the lion apart barehanded as one might*
> *tear apart a kid. But he did not tell his father*
> *or his mother what he had done."*
> —JUDGES 14:6

It seems this was the first time Samson displayed his supernatural strength. We don't know whether he was aware of his power before this moment, but he certainly was fully cognizant afterward, as later events would demonstrate.

After some time, he returned to the vineyard and found honey and bees inside the carcass of the lion he'd killed. During his absence, other wild animals would have picked over the remains of the lion as well. After scraping some honey out with his hands, he ate it while walking to meet his parents. He gave them some but did not tell them where it had come from.

Let's pause here and consider the actions of Israel's soon-to-be champion, the next judge and deliverer of God's people. Samson chose to marry a foreigner, and he defiled himself and his parents by eating honey from the carcass of the lion. Numbers 6:1–21 clearly lays out the stipulations one must adhere to if they are living their life as a Nazirite. One of many adherences was to not touch a dead body or dead animals.

Samson was a willful beast of a young man, dominated by passion, yet God had chosen him before his birth to break the chains of the Philistine oppression.

In Judges 14:10–18, we learn of a feast held by the thirty young men of Timnah, in Samson's honor. Samson displayed his typical brashness once again by posing a riddle for them to solve and attaching a significant wager to it. If the men could solve the riddle in seven days, Samson would give the thirty men two sets of custom-made outfits, one formal and one informal. However, if the men could not solve the riddle, they would have to give Samson thirty outfits, one formal and one informal from each of them. During this period, this was a huge wager and one of significant value. The young men took the bet, no doubt looking to get one over on the Hebrew upstart. When they were unable to solve the riddle, they threatened Samson's wife, telling her that if she did not find out the answer, they would burn her and her father's house. So, his wife sweet-talked Samson into revealing the solution to the riddle. Then she ran straight off and told the men with whom Samson had the bet.

Samson was furious. We already knew he had anger issues by his treatment of the lion. Read the description of how he killed it and consider whether a calm man, a man in control of himself and his emotions, would have done that. The lion did nothing to him, yet he killed it with excessive violence, albeit violence fueled by the Spirit of God. Now, his wife had betrayed him, and the young men had wounded his pride.

> *"Then the spirit of the Lord rushed on him, and he went down to Ashkelon. He killed thirty men of the town, took their spoil, and gave the festal garments to those who had explained the riddle. In hot anger he went back to his father's house."*
> —Judges 14:19

The Spirit of the Lord either caused him to do that or gave him the strength to do it. Either way, God was clearly involved. Afterward, Samson went home, and we are told his wife was given to his best man at the wedding (Judges 14:20). When Samson had calmed down, he went to visit his wife, but was turned away at the door by his father-in-law, who explained that his wife was now someone else's and if Samson was interested in her younger sister, he could have her instead. Samson rejected the offer with the ominous words: "*This time when I do mischief to the Philistines, I will be without blame*" (Judges 15:3). Did Samson mean that he knew he had overreacted last time and was sorry about it?

Samson used foxes to be his torch bearers, tying torches to their tails and sending them into the Philistines' vineyards and olive groves, as well as burning up the standing shocks and grain. He followed up the arson with a slaughter of Philistines. When the men of the town burned Samson's wife and her father alive (Judges 15:6), Samson went nuclear.

> "Samson said to them, 'If this is what you do, I swear I will not stop until I have taken revenge on you.' He struck them down hip and thigh with great slaughter; and he went down and stayed in the cleft of the rock of Etam."
>
> —JUDGES 15:7–8

As smart as Samson was—and he must have been smart to come up with the trick of using the foxes to spread the fire—he did not know how to use either his guile or his physical strength for good. Unfortunately, he used his intelligence as a weapon to humiliate and torture individuals for selfish reasons. As an intelligent man, Samson was probably often bored because there was no one to challenge him physically or intellectually. The state of boredom may have led to Samson entertaining himself by playing these mental games with those who were not as gifted as him.

Samson later killed another thousand Philistine men with a donkey's jawbone after he allowed the men of Judah to bind his hands and turn him over to the Philistines for justice (Judges 15:14–15). After the massacre, which again was assisted by the Spirit of God, Samson was thirsty, so he prayed. This is the first time Samson is recorded talking to God. He first thanked God for his victory—a surprising and perhaps disingenuous act of humility—then he complained about having nothing to drink. God split a rock and provided water for him.

The story of Samson and Delilah is without doubt one of the most famous in the pages of the Bible and has been used in many ways to teach various truths. What can we learn from this sorry tale of a violent, rebellious, and arrogant judge of Israel who went on to fall in love with another Philistine woman by the name of Delilah? Despite popular belief, Delilah was not a prostitute. However, Judges 16:1–3 mentions one occasion when Samson did visit a brothel, so it is reasonable to assume that may not have been the only time.

Once more at the mercy of his passion and hubris, Samson got tricked by Delilah into revealing the source of his great strength. It seems she did it for money, accepting a substantial bribe from some Philistine rulers who were anxious to take their number one enemy out of the picture.

It's interesting to note that Delilah employed the same tactics that Samson's wife had employed—persistently asking him over many days, emotionally manipulating him by suggesting he was only playing with her and did not really love her, until finally she wore Samson down. Whether it was due to guilt or lust, the result was that Samson shared his vulnerabilities and weakness with a woman he felt he could trust, but she betrayed him. Eventually, Samson caved in and revealed the secret of his strength.

> *"So he told her his whole secret, and said to her,*
> *'A razor has never come upon my head; for I have been*
> *a nazirite to God from my mother's womb.*
> *If my head were shaved, then my strength would leave me;*
> *I would become weak, and be like anyone else.'"*
> —JUDGES 16:17

With that confession, God seems to have abandoned Samson. The covenant that had stood between God and Samson since before he was born was broken. Delilah cut his hair while he was sleeping, and when the Philistines came in to capture him, he was unable to resist them. He had lost all of his strength as a result of his choices—in particular, his choice to tell Delilah what should have stayed between him and God.

In captivity, Samson was tortured and had his eyes put out. He was chained to a grinding mill in prison. Up to the time of his capture, Samson had been fearless and unstoppable, a man who had it all and was no doubt the envy of all other men. There is little evidence of Samson's humility aside from that one prayer of thanks at Ramath-lehi following the jawbone massacre. However, in prison, having lost his strength, his vision, the woman he loved, and his freedom, Samson was at his lowest point. Previous disappointments or frustrations had been met with power, but now he was as weak as a lamb. God humbled him by bringing him lower than he would ever have imagined possible. In all likelihood, he felt defeated and ashamed of his choices. He had nothing but time to lament his failings. And God, having opposed his pride, now gave him grace. (James 4:6)

Interestingly, although God allowed Samson's strength to return as his hair grew, He did not restore his sight. We know the outcome of Samson's story, but what must he have felt as new power filled his muscles, while his eyes stubbornly remained useless. How might he have prayed throughout this time? Did he ask for his strength? For his sight? For his freedom? Did he perhaps seek these things so he could exact terrible revenge on the Philistines? Or did he pray for death? The biblical record tells us nothing of that time, and provides no insight into Samson's thoughts, but our speculation is reasonable.

One day, at a great festival held in honor of the Philistine god Dagon, Samson was brought into the temple to put on a show and entertain the crowd. There, for all to see, was the pathetic figure of the conqueror and tormentor of the Philistine people.

> *"When the people saw him, they praised their god;*
> *for they said, 'Our god has given our enemy into our hand,*
> *the ravager of our country, who has killed many of us.'*
> *And when their hearts were merry, they said,*
> *'Call Samson, and let him entertain us.' So they called*
> *Samson out of the prison, and he performed for them.*
> *They made him stand between the pillars..."*
>
> —JUDGES 16:24–25

In Judges 16:28, we see a broken and defeated man once again look to the Lord with his blindness and barren soul. In a twist of fate, when Samson was at his weakest, he was also at his strongest, calling upon the Lord to give him strength to do what needed to be done. One final glorious act, one last demonstration of the power of God, was to come. Samson took hold of the chains, pulled the pillars unto himself, and collapsed the entire structure, killing more than three thousand Philistines in the process. He died and his body was recovered by his brothers and other relatives. They buried him in Manoah's tomb. On that last day of his twenty-year rule over Israel, Samson killed more Philistines than he had during his entire life.

Samson's story is a tragedy. He was an overly emotional man who did not know how to harness his God-given gifts. It appears Samson's parents tried to teach and guide Samson to remain true and faithful; however, like many other men in the Bible, Samson grew to believe that he was much greater than God. His conceit is clear in the biblical narrative. Considering Samson's short life was characterized by many tragic life experiences, including being betrayed twice by women he loved, one may believe his rage was justified at times. From his youth,

Samson had a difficult time controlling his emotions, which took him down a dark path early in his life.

Mastering control over our inner struggles and maintaining emotional equilibrium to steer clear of irrational decisions is undoubtedly one of the most challenging aspects of human behavior. In many cases, individuals succumb to self-imposed urgency, leading to impulsive decisions that lack proper consideration. In my leadership decision-making courses, I often introduce a practical three-step approach to enhance decision-making skills. This method aids in reframing the decision-making process, fostering clarity and sound judgment.

The first step involves introspection: "Is my emotional state high or low?" By acknowledging and categorizing their emotions, individuals can pinpoint the underlying triggers. Notably, heightened emotions often cloud rational thinking, underscoring the need to postpone decisions until a calmer state is achieved. Emotional intensity can serve as a valid reason to delay decision-making until a more balanced mindset is attained.

In the second step, individuals are prompted to ponder, "How will this decision impact others?" This query encourages individuals to assess the repercussions of their choices on those in their immediate circle, fostering empathy and facilitating consideration of both short-term and long-term consequences. This step cultivates a multifaceted perspective, allowing individuals to view the decision through various lenses.

Last, individuals should contemplate, "How will this decision affect me?" Reflecting on the personal implications of a decision, including short-term and long-term effects, is vital for informed decision-making. This step empowers individuals to evaluate their needs, aspirations, and well-being in the decision-making process.

By implementing this technique, individuals can gain fresh insights, uncover unexplored perspectives, and proactively identify potential challenges associated with their decisions. Furthermore, this method facilitates the creation of mental space, enabling individuals to distance themselves from overpowering emotions and fostering a rational decision-making process. I encourage you to leverage this approach during your next decision-making endeavor, as it can pave the way for enhanced clarity and well-considered choices.

Despite Samson's failures, God never left Samson through all his indiscretions. Unfortunately, it was Samson who wandered from God at various times of his life. The only consistency in Samson's life was his inconsistency in following God's plan. Samson was blessed with some of the most amazing gifts that anyone could have ever asked for. His strength and intelligence could have been used to show God's impressive grace and mercy in freeing the Israelites from the Philistines. Instead, Samson left to his own devices, following his own desires, and never really learned to harness the power of his God-given gifts. Jordan Peterson, psychologist and author, has said, *"You should be a monster, an absolute monster, and then you should learn how to control it. It's better to be a warrior in a garden than a gardener in a war."* The truth of the matter is that Samson never really learned to control his inner monster until it was too late. Let us just hope and pray that we can learn to control our own inner monsters before it is too late for us.

Yet, despite his lack of self-control, Samson was still chosen by God in the end. Samson knew what he was doing when he asked the attendant to let him *"feel the pillars on which the house rests"* (Judges 16:26). He also knew what would happen when he pulled on the chains, which means he knew it would end his life. His final prayer is recorded in verse 28, where he asked the Lord to strengthen him just one more time. For all intents and purposes, we see a first indication of what appears to be a suicidal act. Samson was a man who was at his lowest and had lost it all in the end. He had nothing to lose and wanted to die. God answered his request for strength and allowed it to happen because his story and legacy was an important part of God's plan to free the Israelites from the oppression of the Philistines.

Chapter 12

DAVID

A FLAWED MAN, BUT A MAN AFTER GOD'S OWN HEART

David's story is unlike any others in the Bible because David, a lowly shepherd boy, chosen by the prophet Samuel to succeed Saul as king of Israel, is described twice in the Bible as a man after God's own heart—first by Samuel and later by the apostle Paul speaking in the Book of Acts. Much of David's story is well known: his defeat of Goliath, his running battles with jealous King Saul, his ascension to the throne, his many victories in battle, and his fall from grace with a threefold sin that began in his heart as lust. While David certainly faced serious consequences for his sins, God still used David's poor decisions for the greater good of his people.

David was the youngest of eight; all his brothers were bigger, faster, and stronger. The three oldest boys joined Saul's army, but David's size and stature kept him from enlisting. His formative years, it seems, were likely spent in isolation as he tended the flock, cleaning up after the animals and his older brothers, or delivering food and supplies to them. The responsibility for all those menial tasks fell on David's shoulders because he was the youngest, and his older brothers didn't want to do them. It was not all bad for David, though. He developed courage in the face of the wild beasts who tried to attack his sheep, honed his slingshot skills, and would have had a lot of time to speak with God.

He loved music and played the harp so well that he was initially called into the service of King Saul to play the harp for his relaxation. David loved music and did not do "manly or masculine" things. He was clearly different from his brothers in many ways and may not have felt valued, which would have affected his emotional development. The constant mocking and bullying endured by David from his brothers, as well as his own friends or his brothers' friends, may have led to feelings of worthlessness. David always had something to prove to everyone around him. Being bullied at a young age or even picked on laid the foundation for some of his bigger mistakes in life.

Being bullied and ostracized by family members or peers destroys a person's sense of worth, shattering their self-confidence, causing feelings of shame, and leaving them vulnerable to depression or to acting out with violence toward other people. When your identity is based on what other people say about you, you are at risk of succumbing to a dangerous deception. The *lie* is that others define you. Your past defines you. Your circumstances define you. As difficult as this seems, we have to remind ourselves that these lies do not define who we become. This is only true if you allow it to be true. If you accept the lie, it will take hold and destroy you. The remedy is truth. You were made by God for God. You have been created in His image, born to have a relationship with Him. You are defined by God. Your identity is in Him. As we'll see, David was frequently able to live in his own truth and achieve great things, but sometimes he accepted the lie that he was weak—which led to his greatest sin.

After Saul was rejected by God because of an act of disobedience and dishonesty, God sent Samuel to the house of Jesse to identify and anoint a new king (1 Samuel 16:1). Samuel met all of Jesse's sons, figuring, along with everyone else, that the oldest would have been chosen as the future king. He would have been the obvious choice. However, Samuel knew that God's selection for a future king would not be according to the same standards as those set by man. The Lord advises Samuel not to look on the outward appearance but at the heart, as He sees a dark horse in the race for Israel's crown, David (1 Samuel 16:7). David was approximately fifteen to seventeen years of age at the time, had beautiful eyes, and was described as handsome. David was the youngest and smallest of his brothers, but it was he whom God called to be the next king.

No doubt his brothers, perhaps even Jesse himself, wondered about the anointing of David. They may even have doubted the truth of it, refusing to believe the prophecy because it didn't fit with their own beliefs. The Bible says David was filled with the Spirit of God from that day on. This evidently made no difference at all to David's life or how he was treated by his brothers. They may even have made things worse for him, ramping up the ridicule. You... the next king of Israel? What a joke!

When a battle was going to take place between the Philistines and the Israelites, the opposing armies set up camp in their respective corners, waiting to wage war. David's father, Jesse, told David to take food to the battlefield for his three eldest brothers. David would take lunch for his brothers every day, then return home to take care of his sheep. He did this for forty days, each day watching the battle unfold and wanting to help in some way. Day after day, the Philistine champion, Goliath, stomped onto the battlefield to taunt and challenge Saul's army. Eventually, David could not take it anymore. When he looked around and saw all of those powerful and well-armored soldiers, he must have thought: What is wrong with these men? Why won't they go out and just fight? They're soldiers. That's what they do, right?

When David told his brothers that he would go and fight, they laughed at him, of course, as did the other soldiers. Their initial reaction of mockery and shock masked their inner frustration, forcing them to confront their own fear. A mere "boy" was calling them out on their weakness. Not only was Goliath challenging their manhood, but this puny boy was as well. So, they ridiculed David because they couldn't admit their own faults. They scorned his size, his immaturity, and his lack of understanding about warfare.

However, despite the taunting, David's relationship with God meant he knew his own strengths. David insisted on stepping up to take on Goliath. He was undeterred by the many hurtful words spoken against him, and he was fueled by a fire of indignation against his brothers, the other soldiers, and the giant Philistine. He was presented to King Saul, who was in his tent avoiding the embarrassing stalemate on the battlefield. Saul ordered his servants to outfit David with a sword and dress him in the king's own armor. This was probably another attempt to put David in his place. Although it is not recorded in the Bible, Saul, knowing the equipment would be cumbersome and impractical for David, might have said: "So little man, you want to fight the giant? Dress yourself for battle! Don my armor. Wield my sword." David had never used a sword, so even if he had been able to lift it, he would not have known how to use it. Weighed down by the heavy armor, he couldn't move properly; he could barely walk, let alone run.

Despite this further attempt to belittle him, David cast off the armor, dropped the sword, and headed out onto the battlefield armed with nothing but his shepherd's staff and his slingshot. He was woefully outgunned, unprepared in a physical sense, to fight against a heavily armored, seven-foot-tall Philistine. However, David had something the Philistines did not consider. He had the power of God.

When David stepped on the battlefield, he carried five smooth stones that he had chosen from the creek to use for his slingshot. David didn't choose five stones in order to have a backup in case the first stone didn't work. David had a solid trust and faith in God. He knew one stone would be enough. Perhaps the additional four stones were for Goliath's four brothers. David confidently picked those five stones, knowing the purpose for each one, and he walked out to face the giant. Goliath continued to mock the Israelites, saying, *Why do they send a child to fight me?* First Samuel 17:43 records his words: "*Am I a dog, that you come to me with sticks?*"

Consider this for a moment: during the time of this story, the average size of a man was most likely around 5'2" to 5'4". What explanation is there for the presence of a seven- to eight-foot-tall man? It could very likely be the result of additional factors. Goliath had four brothers who were similar in size. It has been scientifically proven that a tumor on the pituitary gland can cause abnormal growth. Goliath and his four brothers, who were all similar in stature, may have reached their extraordinary size because of this. Another medical explanation is gigantism, which is a rare condition causing an excessive growth hormone to be produced in the bodies of children and teenagers.

Irrespective of its cause, abnormal height also leads to poor vision, which is why Goliath said sticks (plural) instead of stick, referring to David's staff.

> *"But David said to the Philistine,*
> *'You come to me with sword and spear and javelin;*
> *but I come to you in the name of the Lord of hosts,*
> *the God of the armies of Israel, whom you have defied.*
> *This very day the Lord will deliver you into my hand,*
> *and I will strike you down and cut off your head;*
> *and I will give the dead bodies of the Philistine army*
> *this very day to the birds of the air and to the wild animals*
> *of the earth, so that all the earth may know that there is a*
> *God in Israel, and that all this assembly may know that the*
> *Lord does not save by sword and spear; for the battle*
> *is the Lord's and he will give you into our hand.'"*
> —1 SAMUEL 17:45–47

Following David's profession of his faith, an almost prayer-like statement, a prophetic statement, he strikes Goliath in the head with a stone from his slingshot, knocking him to the ground. Dead.

It is worth noting that after David killed Goliath, he used the Philistine's own sword to remove his head. Remember how David had struggled to lift Saul's sword? Now, miraculously, he was able to not only lift Goliath's sword, which most likely was bigger and heavier than the one given to him earlier, but he also was able to use the sword to remove Goliath's head. Adrenaline had strengthened him, but God had given him the victory just as David prophesied.

David became the hero of Israel, loved and admired by the people and by Saul, who gave his daughter to David as a reward for his triumph. Eventually David's popularity made Saul extremely jealous, and Saul soon became a petty and vengeful man who chased and hunted the slayer of Goliath. During the long cat-and-mouse game between the two enemies, David had two golden opportunities to end the running conflict, but out of loyalty to the crown—to God's anointed leader—he declined to take Saul's life, insisting it was not right for him to take the life of his king.

When Saul finally died in battle (1 Samuel 31), David mourned both Saul and his son Jonathan, with whom David had a very close friendship. He then went to Hebron, where the people of Judah made him King of Judah and thus began a long war between the House of David and the House of Saul (2 Samuel 3:1). Following the battle of Gibeon and the defection of Abner from the House of Saul, David was anointed king over all Israel, and Jerusalem was designated as the capital city. David retrieved the Ark of the Covenant from Obed-Edom, where it had been entrusted to the care of a Levite family, and brought it back to the new capital city. The procession entered Jerusalem amid much rejoicing, including a celebratory half-naked dance by David, which drew scorn from his wife.

David led his army in a series of victories, but eventually must have grown tired of being on the battlefield. Knowing his generals were more than competent, he left the fighting to them so he could enjoy a more relaxing time at home in Jerusalem. Second Samuel 11:1 states that spring was the time when kings went out to battle. Five ominous words are recorded at the end of the verse: *"But David remained at Jerusalem."*

The first part of David's life seemed to be filled with struggles and constant fights, or surviving being hunted by King Saul. David's decision to stay back from battle when he should have been leading his army can be seen as a moment of weakness and complacency. It is possible that David's success and power as king may have led him to become lax in his responsibilities and duties. This lapse in judgment ultimately led him down a path of sin and moral failure, highlighting the dangers of idleness and the importance of remaining vigilant in one's calling and responsibilities.

Not returning to the battlefield left David with too much time on his hands. One day, he saw Bathsheba bathing on a nearby rooftop. He did not turn away at the first glance, but instead he called for the object of his desire to be brought to him. He slept with her, and she was soon after found to be with child. Bathsheba's husband was on the battlefield when the affair occurred, and although David may have intended it as a one-off, a fling, Bathsheba's pregnancy changed the situation and changed his mind. Whatever his intentions, the result of David making decisions out of lust or out of guilt, or maybe even a combination of the two, was an attempted cover-up of the affair, which ultimately led to Bathsheba's husband, Uriah, being murdered on the battlefield. The complete tale of this unfortunate event can be found in 2 Samuel 11:1–27.

This moment in David's life also seems to be one of the lowest, or perhaps can only be described as despicable. What is rarely ever taught or discussed is the manner in which David was responsible for Uriah's death. Upon finding out Bathsheba was pregnant as a result of their affair, David called for Uriah to return from the battlefield. David began scheming to get Uriah to sleep with Bathsheba so that he could cover up the affair and pregnancy.

Upon returning from the battlefield, Uriah did not go home. Instead he came directly to David, asking in what manner he could serve. David told Uriah to return home and be with his wife so that he could rest. Uriah, surprised at this gesture, told David he could not rest while his men were still fighting. Uriah slept at the entrance to the palace with the rest of the servants rather than going home. The following day, when David learned that Uriah did not go home, he again invited Uriah to the palace and proceeded to get him drunk. Uriah again refused to go home and slept near the palace. Due to Uriah's faithful dedication to his king, David, and honoring his men who were still at war, Uriah was repaid by David in the most atrocious way.

> "In the morning David wrote a letter to Joab, and sent it by the hand of Uriah. In the letter he wrote, 'Set Uriah in the forefront of the hardest fighting, and then draw back from him, so that he may be struck down and die.'"
> —2 SAMUEL 11:14–15

David's actions in orchestrating Uriah's death are indeed a dark and tragic chapter in his life. It is a moment where David's moral compass was severely compromised, and he allowed his desire to cover up his sin to lead him to commit a heinous act. As David wrote the letter to his military commander Joab, instructing him to place Uriah in the front lines of battle, knowing that it would result in his death, it is difficult to ascertain the exact thoughts and emotions that may have been going through his mind. One can only speculate on the inner turmoil he may have experienced in that moment—perhaps feelings of guilt, shame, regret, or even a sense of desperation to protect his own reputation and secure his secret.

Despite his grave error in judgment and the moral failure that led to Uriah's death, it is possible that David may have experienced a deep sense of sorrow and remorse after the deed was done. As a warrior and soldier himself, he may have understood the gravity of his actions and felt a sense of empathy for Uriah, a loyal and honorable man who served him faithfully. In the broader context of David's life, his story is indeed one of complexity and contradiction. He is portrayed as a man of great faith, courage, and leadership, yet he is also shown to be deeply flawed and capable of committing grievous sins. This duality in his character serves as a reminder of the frailty of human nature and the capacity for both good and evil within each of us. During his youth, David may have harbored aspirations of revenge against the bullies who tormented him for his physical attributes. His early experiences of bullying by dominant alpha males shaped his psyche, leading to actions he believed were justified compensation for past grievances. It's as if he were saying, "You once took my toy, and now that I'm bigger and stronger, I'm going to take yours," thus justifying his actions carried out against Uriah. The unfortunate truth is that one deceptive act often begets a series of subsequent deceptions to justify or cover up the initial transgression.

David handed the letter to Uriah to be given to Joab. Uriah, truly trusting his king and top commander, David, unknowingly carried his death sentence by way of the letter. Uriah was ultimately killed exactly how David had planned it. David went on to marry Bathsheba after a short but hopefully respectful enough period of mourning, but God was obviously displeased. The prophet Nathan was sent by God to rebuke David for his sin and let him know there would be serious consequences for his sin.

Nathan indirectly approached the subject with David, perhaps with the intention of giving him a chance to confess his crime and his sin. The prophet told David a story about a man taking a ewe lamb (note how he stressed the sheep was female) from another man because he did not want to kill one of his own lambs to prepare as food for his guest. David listened to the story and then became angry, declaring that the man who did such a thing deserved to die (2 Samuel 12:1–6).

Nathan then gave it to David straight: *"You are the man!"* (2 Samuel 12:7)

It is true that as human beings, we often struggle to confront our own flaws and shortcomings. It can be much easier to point out the faults of others and to justify or rationalize our own actions, especially when they are morally questionable or reprehensible. David's initial inability to see his own guilt in Nathan's parable reflects this common tendency to avoid acknowledging our own sins and mistakes.

The reluctance to confront our own faults stems from a variety of reasons, including pride, shame, fear, and the discomfort of facing the consequences of our actions. Taking responsibility for our errors in judgment requires humility, self-awareness, and a willingness to admit our faults—traits that can be challenging to cultivate, even for someone like David, described as a man after God's own heart.

Despite his initial blindness to his own sins, David's response to Nathan's rebuke demonstrates his capacity for repentance and humility. He acknowledges his wrongdoing, expresses genuine remorse, and seeks forgiveness from God, as evident in his writing of Psalm 51. This pivotal moment in David's life serves as a powerful reminder of the importance of self-reflection, accountability, and the courage to confront our own flaws, even when it is difficult and painful.

The child conceived from David's affair with Bathsheba died, but she later bore him another son. Nevertheless, the difficulty of losing a child will forever leave an unforgettable scar, even after the arrival of the blessing of another child. This blessing did not diminish Bathsheba's pain of losing her firstborn. The memory of the child she had lost must have lingered, a constant reminder of the fragility of life and the depth of her sorrow.

Bathsheba's grief, loss, pain, and suffering are perspectives rarely discussed due to King David's "dedication" to God taking center stage in the biblical narrative. I can only imagine that in the depths of sorrow, Bathsheba wept for her lost firstborn son. Some may cast blame on her for the tragic outcome, attributing it to her past choices. However, I believe that Bathsheba did not actively choose the path that led to her son's demise; rather, she was swept up in the unintended consequences of King David's actions. It serves as a poignant reminder that one person's decisions can profoundly impact the lives of others.

I vividly recall the heart-wrenching moment when I sat beside a mourning mother, her anguish palpable as she coped with the loss of her beloved child. The questions that echoed in her mind—"Why my child?" "Why did God take my baby from me?" "How could this happen?"—were raw and valid, demanding answers that may never come. Though well-meaning voices may offer solace, assuring her that time will heal and wounds will mend, can one truly recover from such a profound loss? Is it fair to harbor anger toward God?

The complex emotions that accompany the loss of a child are not easily resolved. Anger, confusion, and a profound sense of emptiness can linger, leaving one grappling with the fragility of life and the unfairness of it all. The answers, if any, lie in the depths of personal belief and individual experiences. Bathsheba's grief remains a timeless reminder of the enduring human capacity for love, loss, and the search for meaning in the midst of tragedy. It's a story that continues to touch hearts and evoke deep empathy for the complexities of human existence. In Bathsheba's tale of sorrow, the echoes of her anguish still resonate, deeply moving those who encounter it.

Imagine the profound emptiness and shattered spirit Bathsheba must have endured in her grief. Coming to grips with losing such a significant part of her being, with the knowledge that it would never return, must have felt like an interminable torment.

Yet, in His infinite grace, tenderness, and love, God extended His mercy toward Bathsheba. Though the profound pain of losing a child can never truly be erased, God bestowed upon her a second child, offering solace and easing her suffering.

In an amazing, almost breathtaking display of God's compassion, the second son of David and Bathsheba, named Solomon, was born, and he went on to become the greatest of all Israel's kings and the wisest man who ever lived. David's one great sin led to many others, and as Nathan had warned him, trouble never left him during the rest of his days as king. Yet, David is still described as a "man after God's own heart." Luke records Paul's thoughts about David in the Book of Acts.

> "For David, after he had served the purpose
> of God in his own generation, died, was laid beside
> his ancestors, and experienced corruption."
> —ACTS 13:36

Additionally, some of the Psalms David wrote are among the best-known and most widely quoted. Psalm 23, which begins with the well-known line *"The Lord is my Shepherd,"* was written during his time on the run from Saul. After the death of his and Bathsheba's firstborn son, David wrote arguably the best, most sincere psalm of repentance, Psalm 51: *"Create in me a clean heart…"*

You may have been betrayed by your friends or coworkers; you may have betrayed others. You may be stuck in repeating cycles of bad decision-making and bad behavior, making the same mistakes over and over, but remember David, who, after all, was described as a man after God's own heart. Read the Psalms David wrote and feel the deep love he had for his Father in Heaven. He made some terrible mistakes and suffered horribly for them, but God blessed him and used him.

Ultimately, David's story is a testament to the transformative power of God's grace and forgiveness. Despite David's failures and shortcomings, God continued to work through him, using him to fulfill His purposes and demonstrate His redemptive power. David's life serves as a touching example of how even the most flawed individuals can be instruments in God's hands, showing that God's plan can transcend human weakness and bring about redemption and restoration.

Finally, let's not forget that Jesus was a descendant of David, born almost one thousand years after David's death. The Messiah was born in David's city, Bethlehem. Matthew begins his gospel by calling Jesus the son of David. Think about that!

Chapter 13

SOLOMON

TRUE WISDOM DOES NOT ALWAYS AMOUNT TO TRANQUILITY

We've examined several individuals in the Bible so far, but their stories have mostly been told from a third-person perspective. Solomon is different. In addition to the third-person stories told about him, Solomon wrote three books about his life, perspectives, and beliefs: Proverbs, Ecclesiastes, and Song of Solomon. This means his story can be analyzed from his own writings. Solomon's writings present a vivid picture of the man and his relationship with God.

Solomon's defining characteristic is his wisdom, as is evident in both the story about him and his writings. Wisdom has been defined as knowledge applied in the right way at the right time. All the knowledge in the world is useless or even potentially destructive without wisdom, and conversely, wisdom without knowledge is almost like riding a bike without pedals. We are not able to move forward without the proper knowledge for understanding our purpose.

Solomon had all the wisdom he could ask for, but at times he failed to apply it in the correct manner since he was so easily swayed by the women he married. Perhaps Solomon's problem with women was his blind spot—the one area of his life where his wisdom took a backseat. We all have similar blind spots, or weaknesses, some of which we are aware of, others not. Situations in which perfect storms of negative emotions and temptations challenge our resolve. The struggle does not disqualify us from God's grace, nor does failure. Solomon still did great things for God, and we can too, even though the consequences of our sin may be serious and long-lasting.

Solomon was born about 990 BC to King David and Bathsheba. We learned in the previous chapter that Solomon was the second son born to them; their first son had died as a result of King David's choices. As you can imagine, Solomon was both a celebration and fulfillment of a gift given to two grieving parents. Bathsheba truly loved and cared for Solomon, as most mothers do. Since Bathsheba had lost her first son under some terrible circumstances, she certainly was not going to let anything happen to Solomon and would even ensure that he would be David's true heir.

No ascension to a royal throne is without drama, nor is there ever a shortage of political intrigue inside royal families. Although Solomon was not David's eldest son, and therefore not the natural heir to David, God had chosen him. Before Solomon was crowned, Adonijah, his half-brother, got it into his head that he was the man to take over after his father, even going so far as to throw a coronation party for himself. The prophet Nathan intervened, and Solomon was anointed king during Adonijah's party. Stepping into the role of judge and ruler of Israel, Solomon, in his first act of mercy as king, let his half-brother off with a warning (1 Kings 1:52). However, when Adonijah later failed to heed the warning, Solomon had him executed.

Solomon established his reign with the subsequent executions of two of his father's enemies, Joab and Shimei, who were both supporters of Adonijah. Solomon, we are told in 1 Kings 3:3, loved the Lord and walked in the statutes of his father, David. While he offered incense in Gibeon at the principal high place, a place designated for worship, God appeared to him in a dream at night (1 Kings 3:5). The Lord asked Solomon a question, the like of which everyone has surely imagined at some point in their lives—especially those with political power or those seeking it.

> *"At Gibeon the Lord appeared to Solomon in a dream by night; and God said, 'Ask what I should give you.'"*
> —1 Kings 3:5

After responding with praise and gratitude, Solomon asked God for wisdom.

> *"Give your servant therefore an understanding mind to govern your people, able to discern between good and evil; for who can govern this your great people?"*
> —1 Kings 3:9

Much has since been made of this humble request, but if you think about it, it was in fact a logical request. He didn't need to ask for money or power because he had those things already, and many more such blessings would surely come as a result of his wise leadership of God's people. God was very pleased with Solomon's request.

> *"God said to him, 'Because you have asked this, and have not asked for yourself long life or riches, or for the life of your enemies, but have asked for yourself understanding to discern what is right, I now do according to your word. Indeed, I give you a wise and discerning mind; no one like you has been before you and no one like you shall arise after you. I give you also what you have not asked, both riches and honor all your life; no other king shall compare with you. If you will walk in my ways, keeping my statutes and my commandments, as your father David walked, then I will lengthen your life.'"*
>
> —1 Kings 3:11–14

It is interesting to note that when David issued his final instructions to Solomon before his death, he also called him a wise man (1 Kings 2:9). Were these words prophetic? Or merely a statement of fact concerning his son's character? Considering Solomon had everything else, he seemed to know what he lacked at a young age. Without the proper guidance of his father, David, I'm sure Solomon felt he needed wisdom to ensure he was fit to rule Israel as her king.

Solomon's first demonstration of this newly imbued divine wisdom was the case of the two prostitutes. In a nutshell, they each had a newborn child. One of the babies died during the night, leaving a dispute between the two women about whose child had died, and whose was alive (1 Kings 3:16–28). Solomon's judgment was as follows.

> *"Then the king said, 'The one says, "This is my son that is alive, and your son is dead"; while the other says, "Not so! Your son is dead, and my son is the living one."'*

> *So the king said, 'Bring me a sword,' and they brought a sword before the king. The king said, 'Divide the living boy in two; then give half to the one, and half to the other.' But the woman whose son was alive said to the king—because compassion for her son burned within her—'Please, my lord, give her the living boy; certainly do not kill him!' The other said, 'It shall be neither mine nor yours; divide it.' Then the king responded: 'Give the first woman the living boy; do not kill him. She is his mother.'"*
>
> —1 KINGS 3:23–27

The writer of the book of Kings goes on about Solomon's fame in 1 Kings 4:29–34. Solomon surpassed the wisdom of all the people of the East, and all the wisdom of Egypt. He was wiser than anyone. This is reflected in his poetry and philosophical writing. In the Song of Solomon, he showed his youthful side, his passionate pursuit of life to its fullest, and his romanticism. The Book of Proverbs presents the thoughts of a more circumspect, more mature man who has experienced life, both its highs and its lows, and learned from them. Solomon was not just a philosopher, though. He was a warrior and a builder, and once he had established peace by conquering all his enemies, he turned his attention to fulfilling his father's greatest desire: the construction of a temple for the Lord. David had wanted to build the temple and started preparing the necessary materials before the Lord interrupted him. In 1 Chronicles 22:8–10, we read of God's promise to David that his son Solomon would build the temple. When the time arrived for Solomon to realize David's vision, much groundwork had already been laid. Solomon joined forces with the King of Tyre, and

Solomon's Temple, one of the famous temples in ancient history, was built. The project took seven years, and no expense was spared. The very best of materials were used in the construction of the temple. Solomon also built a house for himself, which took thirteen years to construct.

Once the temple was complete, Solomon made a short speech followed by a long prayer of dedication, which in turn was followed by a huge party. In his speech, Solomon spoke of his work as the fulfillment of God's promise to his father, David, by quoting God's exact words to David (1 Kings 8:15–16). Solomon then stated that not only was the temple the fulfillment of God's promise, but he himself was the embodiment of the promise.

> *"Now the Lord has upheld the promise that he made;*
> *for I have risen in the place of my father David;*
> *I sit on the throne of Israel, as the Lord promised, and have*
> *built the house for the name of the Lord, the God of Israel.*
> *There I have provided a place for the ark, in which is the*
> *covenant of the Lord that he made with our ancestors*
> *when he brought them out of the land of Egypt."*
>
> —1 Kings 8:20–21

Solomon's dedication prayer, as recorded in full in 1 Kings 8:22–61, is full of praise and thanksgiving but is also a sermon to the people, reminding them of their responsibilities as God's chosen people.

After eight days of celebrations and sacrifices, Solomon ended the festival, and then sent everyone home. It was at this time that God appeared to Solomon again, as He had done at Gibeon, to tell Solomon face-to-face that He had heard and accepted his prayer. Solomon's fame grew, as did his wealth, such that according to 1 Kings 10:23–24, he excelled all the kings of the earth in riches and wisdom. The whole earth sought the presence of Solomon to hear the wisdom that God had put into his mind.

So far, so good, for the great and mighty king of Israel.

As is the case for many men, Solomon's Achilles heel, it seems, was women. The only time his great wisdom has been called into question is in relation to his choice to marry over 700 women and have about 300 concubines as well. The modern reader will think this is madness, not wisdom. He married many women from different nations even though the Lord had said to the Israelites, *"Do not intermarry with them, giving your daughters to their sons or taking their daughters for your sons, for that would turn away your children from following me, to serve other gods."* (Deuteronomy 7:3–4). And lead him astray, they certainly did.

> *"For when Solomon was old, his wives turned away his heart after other gods; and his heart was not true to the Lord his God, as was the heart of his father David."*
> —1 Kings 11:4

How many men and women throughout the centuries have been led astray by lust, or allowed themselves to be led astray? How many have fallen in the area of sexual purity? How many have been pulled off track by these temptations of the flesh? How many? Many. Perhaps part of Solomon's appeal is not simply his great wisdom, which we still enjoy and from which we still receive rebukes and encouragement, but his humanity. He had everything but he turned his heart away from the One who gave it all to him.

It is likely that Solomon wrote Ecclesiastes as an old man. In Ecclesiastes, Solomon's life can best be described as a time of difficulty, of self-reflection, of questioning and wrestling with wisdom, which he had come to see as a burden. In Solomon's final years, it appears as though the things that would have brought him peace, love, and some form of joy have escaped him. With all the wisdom of the world and the many blessings God had bestowed upon him, he still could not truly identify what joy or happiness looked like. Solomon hadn't found what he was looking for.

God was angered by Solomon's idolatry (1 Kings 11:9), and the almost immediate consequence was the end of peace. God raised up a series of adversaries to challenge and make trouble for Solomon until, eventually, Jeroboam received a prophecy that he was to be given ten tribes of Israel to rule. The prophet Ahijah even told Jeroboam why (1 Kings 11:33). Solomon tried to kill Jeroboam, but he fled to Egypt until Solomon's death, at which time the kingdom of Israel was officially split in two. Solomon's son Rehoboam became king of Judah, and Jeroboam ruled the rest of Israel. The Lord had told Solomon that division would happen, and the reason was that he did not follow the Lord with his whole heart, like his father David.

Solomon was a great king, but like all men, he died. His lasting legacy was a magnificent temple and his three books of wisdom and poetry: The Song of Solomon, Proverbs, and Ecclesiastes. Less positive was the divided kingdom he also left behind. At the onset of Solomon's life and his time as a king, his potential to be a great leader was virtually limitless. He was blessed with one of the greatest gifts God had bestowed upon man, the gift of wisdom. One would think that the wisest man would have known and practiced discernment as a key aspect of wisdom.

However, Solomon began to lose his way as he grew older and perhaps more confident of his own perceived wisdom. In his youthful days, Solomon appeared to be vibrant, appreciative, kind, and compassionate. He was also empathetic, and he seemed to live his life to the fullest. In the Songs of Solomon writings, he professes his love with such descriptive language that you can almost feel the depth of emotion he experienced.

In contrast, in Ecclesiastes we find the great king reflecting on his life as he nears the end. His writings from that time are characterized by sadness and disappointment, describing his failure to find happiness. Others have let him down. He's let himself down too. He even seems to question God's existence.

Solomon's real battle toward the end of his life was to find peace. In Ecclesiastes he asks a series of questions, searching for meaning, wrestling with his experience and knowledge to identify peace, happiness, and purpose. What is it all about? For example, in Ecclesiastes 1:12–14, he writes:

> *"I, the Teacher, when king over Israel in Jerusalem, applied my mind to seek and to search out by wisdom all that is done under heaven; it is an unhappy business that God has given to human beings to be busy with. I saw all the deeds that are done under the sun; and see, all is vanity and a chasing after wind."*

At some point in our lives, we have all asked or will ask that question. As we journey through life, our fortunes will ebb and flow. However, if we can identify what peace and serenity, love, or happiness look like, we have a better chance of achieving it. The search for meaning and purpose is a pursuit that everyone must take seriously. Often, we work so hard to seek what we feel will bring us joy, but once we've achieved "joy" we somehow feel incomplete. We feel let down and unsatisfied, and yearn for more. All these other things—the shiny, sparkly objects—attract our attention with promises they can't keep. However, if we pause from day to day, possibly during moments of prayer, we may want to ask God for the wisdom to truly define what peace and joy look like rather than chasing something that continually changes.

Solomon had everything, but it wasn't enough. He wasn't happy. What makes you think that by chasing after all that glitters in this world, you will be happy? As Jesus said: *"For what will it profit them to gain the whole world and forfeit their life?"* (Mark 8:36)

One key aspect of life I have recently defined and begun practicing is an understanding of the "sense" of three important elements: our sense of direction, our sense of accomplishment, and our sense of purpose. The three must be balanced, and each has to be defined. Oftentimes people will define a sense of purpose and accomplishment, but they lack a sense of direction. Other times we can define a sense of direction and purpose, but we may lack the sense of accomplishment. Balance is the key, and to have a balanced life one must have wisdom. And ultimate wisdom comes from God.

> *"If any of you is lacking in wisdom, ask God, who gives to all generously and ungrudgingly, and it will be given you."*
> —JAMES 1:5

When contrasting the wisdom of the world and what it offers with what God offers, James goes on to say this:

> *"But the wisdom from above is first pure, then peaceable,
> gentle, willing to yield, full of mercy and good fruits,
> without a trace of partiality or hypocrisy."*
> —James 3:17

In the last chapter of his final book, Solomon comes to terms with his mortality and accepts God's will.

> *"The end of the matter; all has been heard. Fear God,
> and keep his commandments; for that is the whole duty
> of everyone. For God will bring every deed into judgment,
> including every secret thing, whether good or evil."*
> —Ecclesiastes 12:13–14

It appears that he turned back to God in his later years, making peace with God and seeing the pattern and purpose of his life. Solomon went to his grave, knowing that despite his flaws, God had chosen him to do great things. Interestingly, Solomon was taken home by his Lord at the young age of only sixty. Hopefully, he found the one thing he could not during his living years: peace, which ironically is the meaning of "Solomon" in Hebrew.

Chapter 14

ELIJAH

THE PROPHET WHO LOST HIS WILL TO LIVE BUT NEVER DIED

The divided kingdom that Solomon left behind was characterized by continual upheaval as the kings of Israel and Judah *"did evil in the sight of the Lord more than all who were before [them]."* (1 Kings 16:30). That phrase is applied with appalling regularity as a footnote to the brief biographies of successive rulers throughout the books of Kings and Chronicles.

God persisted in sending prophets to call these wayward and disobedient kings, and the equally faithless people they led, back to him. Elijah, one of the best-known of these seers, is introduced into the biblical narrative as a Tishbite, from the land of Gilead.

Elijah was able to do some of the greatest miracles recorded. He was visited by God and blessed with some great powers. However, he was still a human, and he had his flaws. When he was mocking the prophets of Ba'al, he was guilty of pride. When he feared for his life, he ran away and hid, rather than call on the Lord to help him. When he lost hope, instead of seeking God, he quit and wanted to die.

There is great value in analyzing Elijah's behavior. One of the most important factors in Elijah's story is found in 1 Kings 19:1–8, a story most applicable to us today. In these short few verses, we find Elijah at his lowest point after having done a great miracle with God's help. Elijah began to focus on all of the negative aspects of his life at that moment rather than focusing on all of the good that had happened.

During this time, the Israelites had become worshippers of Ba'al. Ahab was the king and, according to 1 Kings 16:33, *"did more to provoke the anger of the Lord, the God of Israel, than had all the kings of Israel who were before him."* Ahab married a Sidonian princess named Jezebel and built an altar to Ba'al in Samaria; he made a sacred pole as well. God told Elijah to announce to Ahab that a great drought was coming (1 Kings 17:1). Ironically, Ba'al was considered the god of fertility and rain. As the Israelites worshipped Ba'al, this was again a departure from God and into idol worship. By Elijah delivering this message, Ahab was put on notice that only Elijah's God can deliver rain or life therein.

After delivering the message to Ahab, Elijah was instructed to go hide by the Brook Cherith, which flows into the Jordan River. He was fed by ravens who brought him food, and he was able to drink from the stream. He was then commanded to go and live with a widow in Sidon, where he performed a number of miracles (I Kings 17:8–24). About three years later, God told Elijah to go and visit Ahab again. To make the way easier, God had a man on the inside by the name of Obadiah, who was in charge of King Ahab's palace affairs. Obadiah revered the Lord greatly. Elijah met Obadiah on his way to see Ahab and learned from him that Ahab had been searching for him for years. Ahab blamed Elijah for the drought in Samaria and wanted to kill him. When Elijah asked Obadiah to take him to Ahab, Obadiah refused on the grounds that Elijah might be whisked away again by the Lord, thus subjecting Obadiah to the wrath of his king for saying the prophet had been found when in fact he had not. Elijah promised to show himself to Ahab, so Obadiah agreed to let Ahab know that Elijah was coming to see him.

> *"When Ahab saw Elijah, Ahab said to him,*
> *'Is it you, you troubler of Israel?'"*
> —1 Kings 18:17

The New Century Version of the Bible uses the words "the biggest troublemaker in Israel." Ahab did not like Elijah, even less so when Elijah rejected Ahab's accusation, turning it on him instead, rebuking him for his idolatry.

> *"He answered, 'I have not troubled Israel; but you have, and your father's house, because you have forsaken the commandments of the Lord and followed the Baals. Now therefore have all Israel assemble for me at Mount Carmel, with the four hundred fifty prophets of Baal and the four hundred prophets of Asherah, who eat at Jezebel's table.'"*
> —1 Kings 18:18–19

Once the prophets, and no doubt a crowd of onlookers, were gathered on Mount Carmel, Elijah challenged them all, saying, *"How long will you go limping with two different opinions? If the Lord is God, follow him; but if Baal, then follow him*" (1 Kings 18:21). He then challenged the prophets that worshipped Ba'al to a showdown to see who was the true God. Both groups would prepare an offering, but not light the pyre; rather, they would pray to their god to light it for them. "*The god who answers by fire is indeed God*" (1 Kings 18:24).

Elijah began to show a side of himself he had not shown before. His behavior oddly contradicted what one would expect from a man of God. In fact, it was quite ungodly. As the prophets of Ba'al were cutting themselves and bleeding, possibly to the point of death, Elijah started to mock them and ridicule Ba'al as well. Elijah called out the believers and Ba'al for being too busy or not paying attention. He taunted them, telling them to shout louder because Ba'al might not be able to hear them. Elijah seemed to enjoy making sport of the men as they raved on and slashed themselves. How could a man of God take pleasure in the suffering of others? Knowing that God was capable and would certainly win the contest by answering Elijah with fire, Elijah should have exercised more restraint. He seemed to become carried away with excess emotion, and although we can probably sympathize with this kind of gloating, and perhaps have indulged in similar behavior ourselves on occasion, the sarcastic ridiculing of the prophets of Ba'al seemed to be unnecessary, almost cruel.

When it was clear that the prophets of Ba'al would not be successful, Elijah built his own altar and had the onlookers pour water all over it so that it was soaking wet. Then he prayed to God, and the soaked altar was covered in flame. Once the fire had been lit from Heaven, the people bowed down and worshipped God. Elijah ordered the capture of the prophets of Ba'al and had them taken to Wadi Kishon, where they were executed (1 Kings 18:40).

Elijah then prayed and, as he did, rain clouds formed on the horizon (1 Kings 18:45). Ahab rode his chariot to Jezebel to tell her about the miracle, Elijah's miracle, and to let her know that Elijah had said rain was imminent. Jezebel was not pleased with the news. She was especially angry at Elijah for having all of Ba'al's prophets killed. Remember, Jezebel's influence on Ahab was one of the reasons he and his people began to follow Ba'al. Her response was swift: a messenger was sent to Elijah to threaten him, to warn him that he would soon meet the same fate as her beloved prophets. Elijah was to be hunted down and killed.

Predictably, Elijah took off when he received the message. Again, we see a side of Elijah that is unbecoming of a great prophet. Knowing the extent of God's power and God's ability to protect him—fresh from a great victory on Mount Carmel and with a history of God demonstrating to Elijah His might and His faithfulness—Elijah feared for his life, so he ran away and hid.

This is quite typical of people who suffer depression and anxiety. They may be able to get themselves up emotionally for a big occasion, but it wipes them out, and the low that follows can be deep. Elijah went into the wilderness, afraid for his life, and sat down under a tree and said, *"It is enough; now, O Lord, take away my life, for I am no better than my ancestors"* (1 Kings 19:4). In other words, "I want to die!" Depressed, scared, and discouraged, Elijah wanted to quit life, to lie down and cease his miserable existence.

Elijah was tired, weak, and emotional to the point that he felt he couldn't go on. We know what that feels like. We've had the same or similar feelings during times of loss or difficulty. We may also feel discouraged, and life may seem pointless.

There are many times in our own lives when we lose our way or even lose our will to live. We may also become depressed and sad when the world seems to be against us. In these moments we may feel lost and hopeless. Times like these are often the most difficult to find the strength to believe in God. It's always easier when our life is going smoothly and there seem to be no issues, when all of our bills are paid and we have enough money to make it to the next paycheck. It's easy to be faithful and thankful in good times. However, in those times when all is lost and we find ourselves at our lowest, it's a struggle to find the strength to just go on for one more day. We've all had moments when, like Elijah, we simply wanted to give up, to lie down and sleep and stay asleep so that we didn't have to face our problems.

As he did in Elijah's time of despair, God will also show us the way and help us when we are in need. At his lowest point, when Elijah was ready to die, God continued to protect him. Elijah wanted to sleep an endless sleep, but God had another plan.

> *"Then he lay down under the broom tree and fell asleep. Suddenly an angel touched him and said to him, 'Get up and eat.' He looked, and there at his head was a cake baked on hot stones, and a jar of water. He ate and drank, and lay down again. The angel of the Lord came a second time, touched him, and said, 'Get up and eat, otherwise the journey will be too much for you.' He got up, and ate and drank; then he went in the strength of that food forty days and forty nights to Horeb the mount of God."*
>
> —1 Kings 19:5–8

Whether Elijah responded favorably to the news of a journey or simply wanted the angel to stop pestering him, we don't know, but in either case, he finally got up and traveled for forty days to Horeb, where he spent the night in a cave.

When God finally appeared to Elijah, he asked him what he was doing (1 Kings 19:9). Elijah then had a very personal and intimate conversation with God about his feelings and his concerns, saying that he had worked hard to bring the Israelites back to worshipping God, but had been reduced to running for his life. Basically, he poured his heart out to God. This is just one of many examples in the Bible of honest conversations with God. Sometimes we forget, or choose to ignore, that God knows everything. When we talk to God we hold back, as though we're worried about upsetting Him or concerned that He might be angry with us. Sometimes our own foolish and emotional self-talk gets in the way of trusting Him. We only hurt ourselves when we try to hide from God.

Interestingly, God asked Elijah the same question again, but on the second occasion, it was after Elijah "heard" God in the silence. First Kings 19:11–13 tells us that God told Elijah to stand out in the open on the mountain because He was going to pass by. First came a strong wind, then an earthquake, then a fire, but God was not in any of these. After the fire there was quiet, and it was from within that complete silence, when there were no other sounds or distractions, that God—in a voice variously described as still, quiet, small, and gentle—asked Elijah what he was doing. The repetition was for Elijah's benefit, of course, as God was helping him to focus on the big picture, helping him to see his true calling and purpose.

How often do we truly take the time to slow down and embrace the peace of our own silence? When was the last moment you found yourself "still" enough to simply sit and think? Stillness seems like a long-forgotten concept in today's world, with endless distractions vying for our attention. In a society filled with a plethora of technology, entertainment, and social activities, finding the quiet moments to be present in silence has become a rare luxury. Imagine the benefits of quieting our minds and escaping the constant noise of the world. What if we could use that stillness to have a meaningful conversation with God, much like Elijah did when he could finally hear God's voice in the silence? Amidst the chaos of storms, earthquakes, and fire, Elijah found true connection with the divine only when he slowed his racing thoughts and stilled his tears to listen in the utter quiet.

Elijah answered the question with the same words as before, but something had changed in him because the result of his honest conversation with his Maker, the Lord, was renewal. A renewal of power and a renewal of purpose. God encouraged Elijah, told him his work was not finished yet, then gave him very specific instructions on what to do and who to seek. He was to anoint two new kings, and his own successor.

Imagine Elijah's feelings at this point. He wanted to die, so he ran away into the desert. God woke him up from his depression-fueled slumber, fed him, and sent him to Horeb, where He appeared to Elijah with a personal word of encouragement and purpose. Elijah was full of vigor and ready to go, ready to get back in the thick of the action, to serve the Lord. He heard the names of two men who would be anointed as kings. God then told him to anoint a man to succeed him, to replace him (1 Kings 19:15–17). Was that a punishment or a reward?

Elijah's next mission was to go to Samaria to confront Ahab, who had killed Naboth and taken possession of his vineyard (1 Kings 21: 17–18). When Elijah arrived, Ahab said to him, in recognition of their long-standing feud, "*Have you found me, O my enemy?*" Elijah replied, "*I have found you, because you have sold yourself to do evil in the sight of the Lord*" (I Kings 21:20, RSV). Elijah didn't stop there, though. He pronounced the Lord's judgment against Ahab, telling him that God was going to bring disaster on him and consume him. He added that Ahab's wife, Jezebel, would also die and that dogs would eat her flesh in the street, as a sign of public disgrace. Ahab repented, putting on sackcloth and fasting, and walking around in a sad and discouraged state; this pleased God so much, he accepted Ahab's humble contrition and told Elijah about it (1 Kings 21:29).

During times of despair, discouragement, and sadness, Satan would have us believe that all is lost. He wants us to doubt God's goodness and His providence, and to go it alone or to give up. The Psalmist asked the question, "*Where does my help come from?*" (Psalms 121:1), then answered himself by saying, "*My help comes from the Lord.*" When you are feeling down, look up. Hard times will come, but they will also pass. Through it all God is preparing us for great fights and great triumphs in the future.

In modern times, we have some of the highest numbers of individuals attempting to manage mental health problems. We are dealing with a type of crisis that only seems to be getting worse. Unfortunately, to make matters worse, some of our church leaders believe that if we read the Bible more or pray more, we can solve all of our mental health issues, some going as far as discouraging church members from seeking professional health help from doctors or therapists. When you read the above-mentioned verses, you find a man who is at his lowest and can't seem to find the strength to move on. He falls into a deep sleep, and God sends an angel to look after him. Elijah continues to sleep so much that the angel has to awaken him on two different occasions to force him to eat and drink. It appears as though the angel kept watch over Elijah when he needed it most.

If one of God's greatest prophets, who regularly spoke with God, could not rid himself of the darkness of depression, what chance do we stand? If Elijah could not pray himself out of being depressed, how could a church leader possibly give such hopeless advice? I am not saying that God is not capable of listening to our prayers—prayer can help us through some of our most difficult times. And I am not saying God isn't capable of healing mental health problems. I simply encourage us to reframe our thinking about managing and treating our mental health. Why can't we look at some of our medical staff or therapists as "angels," just as God sent an angel to look after Elijah?

During the workshops I've taught over the years, I often teach various aspects of resiliency, managing stress, and dealing with depression; I've also developed an Emotional Balance Plan (EBP) to assist in those areas of difficulty. An EBP can consist of the following five steps that will guide anyone dealing with stress or PTSD. A proper EBP should include a self-assessment, emotional labeling, creating space, basic physical care, and developing self-control.

Step 1—Self-Assessment: Conduct a self-assessment anytime you are feeling overwhelmed or stressed to assess if your emotional level is high or low. What often happens as a natural process of human behavior is that when your emotional levels increase, your ability to make rational and clear decisions diminishes. Simply put, when emotions run high, rationality runs low. If your emotional levels are high, your follow-up should be to determine why. This process can begin to identify certain emotions you may be feeling, which leads to Step 2. Elijah conducted self-assessment, which is evident in different episodes of his life as he evaluates his actions and motivations. This is particularly noticeable in 1 Kings 19 when, after his victory on Mount Carmel, he flees to Horeb and reflects on his purpose and calling, demonstrating a deep level of introspection and self-evaluation.

Step 2—Emotional Labeling: Once you've conducted a self-assessment, identify what emotions you may be feeling and label those emotions. Each emotion you label will be one step closer to identifying the underlying feelings. By labeling each emotion, we can begin to understand the feelings and why they may be occurring. Additionally, each emotion may be connected to other underlying concerns, thereby increasing the emotionality internally. For example, receiving a pay cut at work may elicit feelings of anger and frustration. Underneath the anger and frustration may be the fear of increasing financial debt, delinquency on the mortgage payments, and inability to fulfill financial responsibilities for the family. And underneath these fears may be the overwhelming fear of loss of empowerment and independence. Emotional labeling is a modern psychological concept, but one can argue that Elijah practiced something similar. He was not afraid to express his emotions to God, whether it was fear, despair, or frustration. An example is when he tells God he feels alone in his mission, expressing his feelings honestly and directly.

Step 3—Creating Space: This is the step where the brain is given time to achieve some clarity by providing physical separation and distance from the stressor and time to process the stress. Often, pausing or momentarily changing the environment can be enough to escalate the recovery process back to a baseline. It may not always be easy to "take a break" in the moment. However, creating space sometime during or after a stressful event can allow the brain to process what has taken place and then internalize the stressor to prevent long-lasting effects. Creating space can be seen in how Elijah often withdrew to solitary places for prayer and contemplation, like when he retreated to the Kerith Ravine and later to a cave on Mount Horeb. These actions show his need for personal space to connect with God and replenish his spiritual strength.

Step 4—Basic Physical Care: Eat healthy, exercise, get enough rest. Of all the steps in this emotional balance plan, this step is possibly the most difficult because the brain is already overtasked and under immense pressure to continue to function. Therefore, attempting to eat a healthy meal when a person is dealing with fear, anxiety, depression, stress, or any other highly emotional event often leads to identifying the quickest and easiest form of food to digest. And when a person is too stressed to sleep, the cause can often be a brain that is under constant pressure and has a difficult time slowing the thought processes down, leading to restless nights of sleep or not being able to sleep at all. Elijah also demonstrated the importance of basic physical care. In 1 Kings 19:5–7, an Angel of the Lord twice wakes Elijah to eat and drink, emphasizing the need for physical sustenance.

If a person is dealing with PTSD or depression, an adverse effect can be too much sleep or not having any energy to complete the simplest of tasks, such as cleaning a room, personal hygiene, getting out of bed, etc. When a person is not able to eat healthily or get a good night's rest, they rarely have the energy to even want to consider exercising.

Scientific research on the effects of exercise on the body has shown it has more of a positive impact on overall physical health than other activities. Exercising even twenty to thirty minutes a day can have positive outcomes on our emotional and physical well-being. Exercise allows parts of the brain to enlarge, such as the hippocampus, which controls learning and memory. The effects of exercise can also lead to eating healthy and a better night's sleep. Create a plan that specifies what time you will sleep, what times you will consciously take a break to eat a meal, and specific times when you will exercise.

Step 5—Developing Self-Control: Often, when I'm teaching classes related to hostage negotiations or crisis negotiations, I teach that there is only one thing we can truly control in a crisis, and that is ourselves and our emotions. Everything else is a perceived sense of control. This holds when we are dealing with any situation in which we may want to effect a change. Elijah had to exercise a considerable degree of self-control, particularly in the face of opposition from King Ahab and Queen Jezebel. Despite threats to his life, Elijah remained committed to his prophetic mission, demonstrating his ability to control his desires and fears in favor of obedience to God. Although he dealt with a deep bout of depression, Elijah did not call upon God to strike down his enemies.

When an individual is dealing with momentary stress, chronic stress, or PTSD, this element of control is an area where we often feel lost. Not being able to control anything in our life, personal or professional, can be a major contributing factor when we are feeling stressed out or emotional. By taking control just in areas where you can, you develop a sense of accomplishment. To begin, you may not be able to control a lot of things regarding work, school, friends, or family issues. However, if you can take control of your sleep, eating habits, exercise, emotions, or a small part of your day, it can begin to shape how you internalize and perceive emotions. Lack of control in one's life can often feel chaotic, even in the simplest of situations. Taking control of yourself is one of the most important factors in dealing with stress or PTSD.

When you feel alone, remember: you are not. You will never be alone. When you feel weak, you are not. God is your strength. At certain junctions in our lives, often primarily due to our own pride or blindness, we may abandon God. However, God will never abandon us. It's often easier to remain at our lowest point, to stay and wallow, to not even try to find the courage to get up off the ground. However, we must remember that it takes greater courage to find the strength we need in our weakest moments. Listen for the still, small voice speaking to you in the silence, speaking words of hope and of life, calling you to get up and follow God.

Chapter 15

JONAH

FAILURE TO LAUNCH

Jonah is one of God's prophets, best remembered for his story of being swallowed up by a whale.

As we read Jonah 1:1–2, we learn that God called Jonah to go to Nineveh to preach to the nonbelievers about God. The Nineveh referred to in these verses was in modern-day Mosul, in Iraq. The Ninevites back in Jonah's day were Assyrians, and Assyrians had a fierce reputation as unfriendly and ungodly barbarians. It's interesting to note that Jonah refusing to go and share God's message was showing implicit bias—Jonah seems to have believed that the Assyrians did not deserve to be saved due to their way of life.

As his first act of disobedience, Jonah boarded a boat in an attempt to escape to a town known as Tarshish. His action appears to not only be a deliberate choice to disobey God's call but may well have also been the last straw for Jonah, who had become sick of preaching to unrepentant people. His years of service trying to call the Israelites back to God had been largely unfruitful, and he was burnt out. Instead of seeing Nineveh as an exciting new mission field, Jonah bailed. After all, if he could not convince his own people, the Israelites, to follow God, how was he going to convince the Assyrians living in Nineveh to follow God? To him, it may have felt like a futile task. So rather than listening and going to Nineveh, he decided to make a run for it, specifically on a boat heading in the opposite direction.

Sometimes we are brought down to our knees in order to listen to God and do His will. No matter how hard we try to run away, sometimes the blessing of being able to prophesy is a heavy burden to carry. It can overwhelm an individual so much that they may feel they cannot go on anymore. Sometimes this is not an indication of lack of faith in God, but rather a lack of faith in oneself, not being able to follow through with such an important call to serve. This deficiency of self-belief can, and often does, interfere with God's calling and purpose for our lives.

Evidently content with his disobedience and apparently having convinced himself that he was off the hook, Jonah was sleeping when a raging storm hit the ship. Everyone on board was freaking out, throwing things overboard to lighten the ship and praying to their various gods to save them from impending doom, but it was to no avail. In desperation, the frantic captain went to wake Jonah up. Maybe he could help. In the captain's opinion, he certainly should have been helping, doing something other than sleeping (Jonah 1:6).

Jonah confessed to the crew that God had told him to go to Nineveh, but he had disobeyed and was attempting to run away. Suddenly feeling guilty, Jonah instructed the men to throw him overboard so that they could be saved. The men protested since he had not done anything wrong, feeling that God would hold them accountable for killing an innocent man. Was it a lack of courage? The other sailors had prayed to their gods to save them, but they were still in danger. When Jonah told the men to throw him overboard, he was in essence also witnessing to the sailors about his God so that they too would come to worship God rather than their own deities. Jonah believed being thrown overboard would result in death; he most likely reasoned that he might as well make his last efforts good. He might as well try to get others to believe in God before he met his Maker. Keep in mind that we never know when opportunities may arise for us to share our testimony of salvation with those who may need to hear it, even if it's our last act before we take our final breath.

When the fearful mariners finally threw Jonah overboard, the storm immediately ceased, causing the sailors to fear God even more. Jonah 1:16 tells us that their response to being saved from the storm was to make a sacrifice to the Lord and make vows to Him.

God provided a large fish to swallow Jonah whole and thus save his life. As there seems to have been no resistance offered by Jonah, it is possible that as soon as he hit the water, he passed out and remained unconscious until he was swallowed up.

What a feeling it must have been for him to wake up to the vile smells and various sounds inside the stomach of the fish. He probably had very little room, or none at all, to move. There would have been no light. I wonder if, initially, when he realized he was alive, he wished that he were dead. His first two thoughts must have been, *Am I dead?* and *Where am I?* It may have taken him a while to calm his brain, come back to reality, and recall the last few minutes of his life. Keep in mind that stomachs contain various acids that are produced to break down food. These same stomach acids could have resulted in a very painful experience for Jonah. Or did God also protect him from that?

Upon realizing he must be in the belly of a fish, Jonah's first course of action was to pray to God and ask for help, to seek solace, to beg for release or maybe death. Can you hear Jonah crying out to the Lord, saying, "Why didn't you just let me drown, Lord? What is this prison? This torture chamber? Get me out of here or kill me, please!"

> *"I called to the Lord out of my distress, and he answered me; out of the belly of Sheol I cried, and you heard my voice."*
> —JONAH 2:2

Jonah was in pain, feeling hopeless and helpless. However, he still turned to God, and through all of his suffering, he was reminded of God's great powers. Some may look at these verses and believe that Jonah died and was brought back to life. However, I believe, based on his cries for help, that Jonah needed to be reminded that God would be there for him through all of his pain and suffering. It surely also served as a warning to Jonah that the next time God asked him to do something, he may want to listen rather than attempt to escape.

Some of you may have experienced what are commonly known as sensory deprivation tanks or salt floats. It's dark inside them and you feel weightless. After a while, you don't even know which way is up or down. Picture being trapped in a confined space, blind and weightless, but also overwhelmed by the most foul smell you could ever imagine. That was most likely Jonah's experience for three days.

Only one of Jonah's prayers is recorded in the book, but they must have been endless during his waking hours, assuming he could sleep. Remember where Jonah is and what he has endured, yet his prayer is a prayer of thanksgiving, at the end of which the Lord commands the great fish to spew him onto dry land (Jonah 2:10).

God knows there is a purpose for each of us to serve. Sometimes we are too busy trying to suffocate those voices and deal with all the distractions rather than doing God's will, like Jonah, who must have gone through a very torturous time in the belly of the fish for three excruciating days and nights. Not being able to see anything, only feeling the movement of the fish and the sting of the painful stomach acids, Jonah did not know when or how he would escape that prison. When would his intense physical and emotional suffering end? It was worse than any pain he had ever endured, and he didn't know when it would stop. If he had listened to God the first time, he would not have had to endure so much pain and suffering. Jonah only hurt himself by being disobedient.

When God commanded Jonah a second time to go to Nineveh, once he had been "vomited" out of the fish's mouth, he went without any objection. Jonah's knowledge of God was, like ours, finite. He could not truly understand God's mercy and His saving grace against all odds.

Jonah arrived in Nineveh and began to preach to the people, prophesying that Nineveh would be destroyed in forty days if the people did not ask for forgiveness. Let's pause here and examine these few words. God had instructed Jonah to preach a message to the people of Nineveh. Although Jonah had suffered through and survived his time in the belly of the great fish, for some reason he still seemed to hold certain anger, frustration, and even bias against the Assyrians. Jonah may have felt the Assyrians did not deserve to be saved since they were enemies of the Israelites. If the Assyrians converted and followed God, what would that mean for his people? Jonah would have rather been preaching to his own people than those he considered his enemies.

Unfortunately, this level of animosity or anger is unlikely to remain hidden. You can be sure it will rear its ugly head at some stage. I have always wondered whether God would have used force or violence to get the people of Nineveh to follow Him, or did Jonah take some liberties in adding in his own message of destruction of the city to scare the people into believing? Either way, the message was delivered, and the Assyrians heard it. The reaction was phenomenal.

Much to Jonah's surprise, the people of Nineveh began to believe. (Jonah 3:5) They believed the message and repented, calling for a fast and dressing themselves in traditional robes of contrition: sackcloth. When news of this move of God over Nineveh reached the king, he too repented in sackcloth, making a decree that the whole city, including all the animals, should fast and wear sackcloth. Even the animals! To avoid the wrath of the Almighty, the king of the Assyrians would take no chances. The people were told to cry out to God for mercy and to turn from their wicked and violent ways (Jonah 3:8).

Imagine what that sight must have been like, three thousand years ago, when Jonah preached a message of salvation to those who desperately needed to hear it. The people believed in God and genuinely repented, and God forgave them. What a celebration it must have been. What joy Jonah must have felt. The mass conversion of an entire city who believed in the Almighty God. Jonah must have been delirious with excitement, and praise must surely have burst from his lips. Not so. Not even close. The salvation of the Ninevites was met with contentious and disappointing behavior by Jonah, who showed his true colors.

> *"But this was very displeasing to Jonah, and he became angry. He prayed to the Lord and said, 'O Lord! Is not this what I said while I was still in my own country? That is why I fled to Tarshish at the beginning; for I knew that you are a gracious God and merciful, slow to anger, and abounding in steadfast love, and ready to relent from punishing.'"*
>
> —Jonah 4:1–2

Jonah said that if he was left in his country, maybe he could have been able to convince other Israelites to believe in God, or to turn back to God, rather than those who did not deserve it. The pain of seeing the people of Nineveh repent and believe was too much for Jonah. In a strange prayer, he praises God for being gracious, merciful, and slow to anger while at the same time criticizing Him for displaying those very qualities to the Ninevites. He was so upset about it that he became physically ill and depressed and asked God to let him die. What would have been considered a success in everyone else's view was deemed a failure by Jonah. Let's call this behavior out for what it really was: pure racism. Jonah did not believe the Assyrians were worthy of God's grace and mercy.

Jonah was chosen for his abilities to be a prophet; however, that also became his biggest flaw once he stopped listening to God. Despite his disobedience, petulance, and blatant racism, Jonah was used by God to bring salvation to the whole city of Nineveh. Don't ever think He can't use you, too.

After Jonah had finished complaining, he stomped out of the city and sat down to sulk. In another act of grace, the Lord appointed a bush to grow over Jonah to provide shade for him (Jonah 4:6), but the next day God took it away. Jonah once again became angry and wished to die since it was too painful to sit in the heat without shade. God then rebuked Jonah, telling him that he felt pity for the tree, which was something he did not work for or even care for. The people of Nineveh were far more valuable than the tree and way more important than Jonah's discomfort. According to God, they were like children who did not know their left from their right, and He challenged Jonah to consider how much more He, the Lord, should care for them.

Jonah's job was to preach to the Ninevites about God's grace. However, much like his predecessors, he made the entire experience about himself rather than about God. How quickly Jonah forgot the miracle of his three days and nights in the belly of the fish. How easily he assumed he knew better than God, and how readily he became a judge rather than a vessel for God's message of mercy. If it wasn't so shockingly childish and racist, Jonah's behavior would be comical. Yet God knew Jonah when He called him to prophesy, when He sent him to preach love to his enemies.

If there is a question mark over Jonah's existence and whether he was a prophet who was swallowed up by a great fish, it can be put to rest by Jesus Himself. If you believe that every word that Jesus spoke was true and you consider it to be the word of God, then Jonah's story must be true because Jesus references Jonah in Matthew 12:40 and Luke 11:30. Jesus talks about His calling to serve and forecasts His death and resurrection by comparing Himself to Jonah spending three days in the *"belly of the sea monster."*

Chapter 16

DANIEL

LIVING A LIFE WORTH DYING FOR

The remarkable story of Daniel is about a man whose life was marked by extraordinary encounters, divine revelations, and steadfast devotion to his God. Daniel's story, in its truest form, is about a man betrayed by those he trusted, those he worked side by side with, perhaps even considered his friends. Through many trials and tribulations, he remained a beacon of unwavering faith and unparalleled wisdom. Although the Bible does not highlight any specific flaws Daniel may have had, the reality is that we are all flawed, including Daniel. Daniel's absence during a particular difficult time for his three friends does not particularly put one of our biblical heroes in a great light. Daniel had also risen to such prominence for the kings that he had advised; however, he failed to utilize that leadership position to stand up for others. Though others may see it as a courageous act of faith or dedication, perhaps Daniel could have avoided the unnecessary risk of praying with the windows open by knowing his surroundings. His daily invocations to God could have continued if he simply would have paid attention to those around him. Although the Bible may not specifically highlight Daniel's flaws, we can still evaluate his actions and analyze his behaviors displayed during those particular times.

From his early years in Jerusalem to his rise in the Babylonian court, Daniel remained resolute in his commitment to God, even in the face of adversity. His unwavering faith and God-given wisdom not only preserved his life but also impacted the lives of those around him. Daniel's unwavering faith and devotion to God came at a price. He became isolated and divided from his peers. His division from the world brought him closer to God; however, he could still have used his testimony to strike a balance by witnessing to others.

As foretold by Isaiah several generations earlier, the Kingdom of Judah was overrun by her enemies (2 Kings 24:1) during the reign of Jehoiakim. First Egypt, then Judah, fell in fulfillment of what the Lord had said regarding punishment for the sins of Manasseh. Jehoiakim's son eventually surrendered to Nebuchadnezzar, King of Babylon, who stripped Jerusalem of all its treasure and all the officials, warriors, artisans, and smiths—ten thousand captives in all (2 Kings 24:14). Only the poorest people remained.

At approximately seventeen years of age, Daniel was one of those taken away from his home and into slavery. After Jehoiakim's surrender, King Nebuchadnezzar ordered his chief of staff, Ashpenaz, to choose some of the best and brightest from Israel so that they could be trained up properly to serve the king. They were to be educated in the Babylonian system for three years, taught the language and literature of the Chaldeans and trained to be fitting servants in the Babylonian court. In Daniel 1:4–6, we learn that Daniel and three others were chosen specifically for their intelligence, maturity, and good looks. They were also quick to learn tasks and feared God.

The specific characteristics Daniel was chosen for were the same characteristics that made him so special. His innate ability and unconditional service to God meant that Daniel had a special relationship with God and was chosen to do His will under some of the most difficult conditions, and the trials came early in his time in the palace. An interesting facet of Daniel's life was that he was chosen, as noted above, because of his good looks and intelligence, much like the reasons Esther (whom we'll discuss in the next chapter) was chosen as a potential wife for King Ahasuerus. Given their similarities, it's interesting to compare how Daniel used his influence versus Esther using her position to save the Jews. An article written by Morgan Smith and published by CNBC in February 2024—"Men benefit more from their looks at work than women do, new research shows"—discusses the double standard set when men and women use physical appearance in the workplace. Even in modern times, if a woman uses her physical beauty or intelligence to effect a major change, she can be categorized as "difficult" or "bossy," as opposed to men who behave the same way, who would be considered strong leaders or confident. This double standard was even being played out in biblical times. And Daniel certainly seemed aware of how special he was.

Upon arriving in Babylon, Daniel was told what to do—what to eat and drink so that he could be trained to serve the king in the proper manner. Daniel's first test was to stand up to the demands that directly contradicted his beliefs. How often are we tested in our lives, whether in our professional or personal lives, when we are told or instructed to go against our beliefs for the "greater good"?

Daniel first resolved not to defile himself with the royal rations of food and wine to which he was entitled. This is an important early indication that Daniel is a man of principle and courage. After he decided not to eat the rations, he had to make his intentions known to the king's men. Daniel approached the palace master to ask that he not be forced to defile himself. We should note that if Daniel did not eat the rations and became unwell or weak as a result, it would have spelled trouble for the palace master (Daniel 1:10). Daniel came up with an alternative, a solution to the problem. In a bold act of faith, he proposed a ten-day trial period, during which he and his companions would consume only vegetables and water.

Daniel then said, *"You can then compare our appearance with the appearance of the young men who eat the royal rations, and deal with your servants according to what you observe"* (Daniel 1:13).

It was a sensible suggestion, which Daniel delivered with humility, and miraculously, at the end of the trial, he and the other young men appeared healthier and more robust than those who had indulged in the king's delicacies. This demonstration of God's favor not only spared Daniel from compromising his faith but also earned him the respect and admiration of his captors. Unfortunately, individuals who frequently lack essential nutritional provisions or basic life necessities may exhibit a pattern of overindulgence when those needs are suddenly met. This behavior stems from the uncertainty of when these provisions will be available again, creating an unhealthy relationship with food or other basic necessities. Recognizing and understanding one's physical needs and how to fulfill them effectively can promote a healthier lifestyle.

Despite his youth, this single act displayed great wisdom to the king and his men. The value of self-care before service to others was an important part of Daniel's testimony. His message of healthy eating and self-care reflected his devotion to God. If he lived a life worth living for God, then it was certainly worth dying for.

As Daniel's reputation grew, so did the challenges he faced. Nebuchadnezzar, troubled by a series of perplexing dreams, sought an interpreter who could unravel their meaning. The wise men of Babylon, renowned for their supposed powers, failed to provide the answers the king sought. However, Daniel, relying on his unwavering faith and God-given wisdom, stepped forward and revealed the dreams' interpretations (Daniel 2). This extraordinary feat elevated Daniel's status in the Babylonian court, positioning him as a trusted advisor to the king.

Nebuchadnezzar fell on his face and worshipped Daniel (Daniel 2:46). Daniel seemed to accept this adoration even though the king's praise was directed at God. Prostrating before Daniel and ordering grain and incense offerings for him were clear acts of worship, which Daniel said nothing about. Perhaps it would be helpful to consider Peter's response in a similar situation, when Cornelius bowed to worship him (Acts 10:25–26), or the angel's words to John in Revelation 22:9: *"You must not do that! I am a fellow servant with you…"*

It seems that Daniel may have been consumed by pride, potentially feeling overwhelmed by the situation at hand. Evidence of his mental state can be found in Chapter 3 of Daniel. In the previous chapter, Daniel had successfully secured positions of authority in Babylon for his friends Shadrach, Meshach, and Abednego, yet interestingly, their Hebrew names were changed to Babylonian names upon their promotion. Despite this, Daniel chose to retain his Hebrew name, even after being appointed as "chief prefect over all the wise men of Babylon," a title that granted him significant influence and power as the primary advisor to the king. With this new role, Daniel would have been privy to all the happenings in the kingdom, including the construction of a large golden statue.

Instead of considering the well-being of his friends, Daniel seemingly focused on himself. He had the power to request that his friends retain their Hebrew names, but he did not. How did he feel when King Nebuchadnezzar prostrated himself before him? It is evident that Daniel's rise to power brought about a shift in dynamics, raising questions about his motivations and the impact of his newfound authority.

Shadrach, Meshach, and Abednego are famous because they were thrown into a fire as punishment for refusing to worship a golden statue of Nebuchadnezzar. They not only miraculously survived but were not hurt at all (Daniel 3: 1–30). The question arises here: where was Daniel? Did he escape the fate of his friends because he bowed down to the idol? That seems unlikely, given what we know of Daniel. Did he avoid punishment because of his rank? Did he pull some strings in the palace? We don't know. However, Daniel's absence in the events described in chapter 3 arouses suspicion. He was not punished, but neither did he stand up for his friends.

Daniel would certainly have known what happened, and that the accusations against Shadrach, Meshach, and Abednego were false, yet he is completely absent. At best, we can hope he prayed for them, but surely he had the power to keep them from being thrown into the fire in the first place. So where was he? Was it pride? Fear? Politics? Whatever it was, there seems to have been no consequences. We can only assess what we read, and it looks like Daniel abandoned his friends when they needed him!

We may wonder at Daniel's deserting of Shadrach, Meshach, and Abednego, but in the overall scheme of things, the incident brought great glory to God. We should take heart again from this: God will still use those who are guilty of sin and poor judgment. Faithful believers do not get disqualified from service.

This fault was overlooked by God in an unsurprising act of grace. However, we know that God does not like pride, and he sometimes punishes it severely. King Uzziah was struck with leprosy, for example, and Nebuchadnezzar himself, in an alarming fall from grace, went mad and lived in the wild like an animal for a season. (Daniel 4:28–33). Daniel received no such punishment. In fact, the king showered him with gifts and promoted him to ruler of the province of Babylon and chief prefect of all the wise men (Daniel 2:48).

In Daniel 4, King Nebuchadnezzar has a dream where he sees a great tree that reaches to the heavens and provides food and shelter for all creatures. However, an angelic watcher declares that the tree will be cut down and its branches stripped away, leaving only a stump.

Daniel, upon hearing the dream, is scared because he knows that it foretells a judgment upon the proud and arrogant king: The king will live like a wild animal, eating grass and living outdoors, until he acknowledges that the Most High God is sovereign over all kingdoms and gives them to anyone He wishes. Daniel is afraid of the consequences that the dream holds for Nebuchadnezzar and his kingdom, and avoids interpreting the dream for "a while." The Bible doesn't specify how long "for a while" exactly was, but it's possible Daniel avoided the king after hearing the recount of the terrible dream. He may have asked for time to pray about what it meant. Or he may have stood there in the presence of Nebuchadnezzar and simply been too afraid to open his mouth. In any case, the king encourages Daniel to not be afraid and to tell him the meaning of the dream. Some of Daniel's final words to the king were "*… your kingdom shall be re-established for you from the time that you learn that Heaven is sovereign*" (Daniel 4:26). Then he told the king to repent, to atone for his sins, and to be merciful to others.

So, it seems the reason for Daniel's reaction was either his affection for the king or fear that the king would kill him because of the interpretation, blaming Daniel for it.

Ultimately, the dream comes true as Nebuchadnezzar is humbled and driven away from his kingdom, living like a wild animal until he acknowledges the sovereignty of God. This episode highlights the importance of humility and recognizing God's authority in all aspects of life.

Eventually, the kingdom was taken over by sixty-two-year-old Darius the Mede, also known as Cyrus, the king of Persia.

During the reign of King Darius, Daniel's rivals discovered that he, having "*distinguished himself above all the other presidents and satraps*" (Daniel 6:3), was to be promoted to number two in the land. Jealous, they conspired against him (Daniel 6:4), manipulating King Darius into issuing a decree that prohibited prayer to any god or man except Darius himself. They knew that attacking Daniel in relation to his faith was the only way to get at him because his performance in his job and his life was faultless, and he had the favor of the king. The king signed the decree written by Daniel's enemies. Worship of or prayer to any divinity was outlawed for thirty days. The law came with a punishment: death in a den of lions. Unfazed by the threat of punishment, Daniel continued to pray openly to his God.

Daniel had a prayer room in his house, and there he went to pray three times a day, facing toward Jerusalem, with the windows open. He continued this practice every day, just as he had his entire life. Daniel would obey every law except any that caused him to give up his daily communion with God. Remember too: he did not pray in secret. He opened the windows of his home so that anyone could see. Daniel knew the risks of his actions and what it meant to continue his faithful worship of his God.

As intelligent as Daniel was, he may have also become complacent because of the repetitive behavior: three times a day at the same time in the same place. Had this become a meaningless ritual? Did Daniel need to flaunt his piety? Knowing there were risks attached to his worshipping schedule, Daniel seemed to not look back or take any precautions in ensuring he would not be caught. Leaving the windows open, knowing that he could be seen by others, appears to be what we in my profession call "poor OpSec" (operational security) or "lack of situational awareness." All of his behaviors prior to his time of prayer every day certainly seemed to show he lacked awareness of his surroundings. Was this boldness or arrogance? The ban only lasted thirty days—surely he could have been less obvious about his civil disobedience.

On the other hand, he may simply have refused to make any concessions because he believed he was in the right. His no-compromise approach, despite knowing all of the consequences of his actions, was perhaps a declaration of confidence in the Lord rather than smugness. But we are to remain diligent and good stewards in ensuring our safety and the safety of others and avoiding unnecessary risks. Safety should be a part of our stewardship.

Those same individuals who knew that Daniel would not worshipping his God followed him home and spied on him. Once they'd witnessed Daniel's crime, these petty and envious men went straight to the king. Imagine their delight in bringing this news. Their plan had succeeded. They must surely have said to themselves, "Daniel has only himself to blame."

Naturally, Darius was not happy with the report and was upset knowing that one of his most trusted men was guilty of stubborn disobedience. In fact, Daniel 6:14 says Darius was distressed and tried desperately to get Daniel off the hook. Unfortunately, as the conspirators repeatedly pointed out to him, he had no other option but to follow through with a proper course of action. The law was the law. There were no exceptions, which meant Daniel would be cast into the lion's den. Darius was there when Daniel's sentence was carried out, and he wished Daniel well: *"May your God, whom you faithfully serve, deliver you!"* (Daniel 6:16)

And deliver him, God did. King Darius rushed to the den early the following morning after a sleepless night of fasting for Daniel (Daniel 6:18–19). Darius called out to Daniel, who replied in verses 21 and 22. God's divine intervention preserved Daniel's life, and he emerged unharmed from the jaws of the ferocious beasts. After Daniel was removed from the lion's den, the king ordered that his accusers be brought, together with their families, and thrown to the lions. Darius then issued a new decree telling everyone in the kingdom to worship the God of Daniel (Daniel 6:26–27). Wow! Talk about influence in high places.

When we look back at our lives, I'm sure we can recall a time or two when we were betrayed by our own trusted friends or fellow coworkers. People close to you, who knew you, yet still took advantage of your vulnerabilities. As Daniel trusted God and continued to worship Him daily without due regard for the consequences, his punishment, in the eyes of those who betrayed him, may have been justified. If this was brashness or arrogance by Daniel, God nonetheless had a plan. While others had mistaken Daniel's efforts as criminal, God used those same actions to display His glory by saving Daniel from certain death.

Though many people only know about Daniel through the story of the lion's den, his work was far from over as he got older and began serving King Belshazzar. Daniel had two terrifying visions during Belshazzar's reign (Daniel 7 & 8). The final one was ultimately interpreted for him by the Angel Gabriel (Daniel 8:15–17). Daniel was traumatized by these visions and must have wished for them to stop. In verse 27 of Chapter 8, we read that he was *"overcome and lay sick for some days."* He recovered and went back to work but was still troubled by what he had seen and perplexed as to the meaning of the vision. Daniel carried this burden for some time because it was not until a new king was crowned that Daniel was finally given understanding.

He decided to seek an answer from the Lord by prayer and fasting. He prayed a wonderful prayer of contrition for himself and the people of Israel. While he was praying and confessing his sin, Gabriel appeared to him again, and told him what the vision meant (Daniel 9:21).

This pattern of prayer, visions, prophecies, and more prayer characterized the later years of Daniel's life. He was often unwell and frequently went without food. He says in Daniel 10:8 that, after seeing another vision, his strength left him and his complexion became deathly pale. He even complained to Gabriel.

> *"My lord, because of the vision such pains have come upon me that I retain no strength. How can my lord's servant talk with my lord? For I am shaking, no strength remains in me, and no breath is left in me."*
> —Daniel 10:16–17

Gabriel then touched him, encouraging and strengthening him. His final words to Daniel, at the completion of the last Messianic vision, were, "*Go your way, and rest; you shall rise for your reward at the end of the days*" (Daniel 12:13).

Despite the terror they caused Daniel and how weak and ill he became because of them, these revelations, recorded in the Book of Daniel, unveiled the rise and fall of empires, the coming of the Messiah, and the ultimate triumph of God's Kingdom. Through these visions, Daniel's faith and understanding of God's plan deepened, providing hope and reassurance to future generations.

Daniel's testimony was not always received positively by those whom he worked with. He had been "promoted" at an early age and continued to do well in his high-ranking position, but that aroused jealousy and animosity in those he trusted, which resulted in some painful times. Imagine his thoughts as he sat overnight in that pit with those lions. Imagine the burden of betrayal.

Daniel's story continues to inspire believers today, reminding us that in the midst of trials, our faith can shine brightly, and God's wisdom can guide us through the darkest of times. God can even permanently close the mouths of those beasts that intend to harm us.

Chapter 17

ESTHER

AN UNDERCOVER AGENT FOR GOD

Very rarely do people ever consider or read a story in the Bible and relate it to a good spy novel. After all, the Bible is written in text that can be very difficult to read or parables where stories can be interpreted multiple ways based on an individual's personal needs, experiences, or life skills. Consider how often we have looked at a character in the Bible where the true hero…is a woman! Their male counterparts are often elevated to hero status regardless of their major flaws or poor decisions.

Around 483 BC, in the kingdom of Persia, there lived a young Jewish girl named Esther. She was an orphan. Raised by her uncle Mordecai, who loved her as his own daughter, Esther possessed a rare beauty that captivated all who beheld her, but her true beauty lay within her heart, where kindness, courage, and unwavering faith resided. In this chapter, you will read a unique story about a powerful and faithful woman who risked everything to save her people. Esther is one of only two women, Ruth being the other, who has her own book included in the biblical canon. There are sixty-six books in total, but only two bear the names of women. It is safe to assume that these books have something special to teach us. Additionally, there are only two books in the entire Bible that do not mention God directly—Esther and Songs of Solomon. However, God was present every step of the way in these two books.

Esther's role as it is portrayed in the Bible can be compared to that of an undercover agent in several ways. Just like an undercover agent, Esther had to conceal her true identity and purpose while navigating a dangerous and complex political environment. She went through a process of preparation and training before entering the king's court, similar to how undercover agents undergo extensive training before being deployed on a mission. Esther had to use her intelligence, wit, and charm to gather information, gain the trust of key individuals, and ultimately achieve her objective of saving her people. This required her to constantly assess risks, make strategic decisions, and maintain her cover under intense scrutiny. Similarly, undercover agents must rely on their skills of deception, persuasion, and quick thinking to accomplish their mission objectives while facing potential threats and adversaries. Esther also experienced emotions commonly associated with undercover agents, such as fear, anxiety, loneliness, and an identity crisis. She risked her life by approaching the king without being summoned, knowing that she could face severe consequences for her actions. Esther's bravery and willingness to take risks for the greater good mirror the sacrifices made by undercover agents who put themselves in harm's way to protect others and achieve their goals.

While Esther is undoubtedly a commendable hero, spy novels often depict undercover agents as individuals who must sometimes compromise their beliefs or go against their true character to achieve their objectives. For example, due to her role, Esther may have had to make difficult decisions that conflicted with her faith. However, in doing so, she was able to ultimately achieve a greater good by saving her people.

Throughout the last thirty years of being in law enforcement, I have had the blessing and the curse of working on various types of violations and investigations. Also during this time, I too found myself either working in an undercover capacity or creating various backstories for my interactions with certain subjects or suspects. Much like Esther, I have had to adopt various identities for various missions or calls for service. Each identity left an indelible mark, and I learned something from each experience. However, the physiological responses during those moments were always the same: angst, adrenaline, excitement, and a little bit of fear to heighten the senses to ensure survivability or success in a mission.

> *"This happened in the days of Ahasuerus, the same Ahasuerus who ruled over one hundred twenty-seven provinces from India to Ethiopia."*
> —Esther 1:1

During this time period, the first remnant of Jews who had returned to Judah were struggling to reestablish temple worship according to the Law of Moses. But Esther and Mordecai, along with many other Jews, had chosen not to make the trek back to Judah. They seemed content to stay in Susa, the capital city of Persia, in which the story is set.

In the third year of his reign, Ahasuerus held a huge banquet for all his officials and ministers, most likely to celebrate himself. When it was over, he held another banquet for the residents of Susa, the capital city of his empire and his home. That feast lasted seven days. Ahasuerus's wife, Queen Vashti, held a concurrent feast for all the women. On the last day of the feast, King Ahasuerus was drunk, and he ordered his eunuchs to bring Vashti to the palace so that he could show her beauty to everyone (Esther 1:11). She refused, which naturally made King Ahasuerus very angry. He sought advice from his most trusted men, who made the harsh recommendation to replace Vashti with a new queen. The impetus of their argument was, once the women of the kingdom had heard how the queen treated the king with contempt by refusing his request, other women in the kingdom would all follow suit and begin some kind of rebellion against not only the men in their lives, specifically their husbands, but also against the king's officials.

Vashti was therefore forbidden from entering the king's presence and would be stripped of her crown as soon as a suitable replacement was found—a better woman (meaning more compliant). We read in Esther 1:21 that the men's advice pleased the king, so he issued a royal decree. The decree was sent to every home in every province in multiple languages, saying that *"every man should be master in his own house"* (Esther 1:22).

A harem of virgins was selected and brought before the king; the one who pleased him most would be chosen to be the new queen (Esther 2:4). Esther was one of the young women chosen. According to palace regulations, the women had to spend twelve months preparing themselves to meet the king, during which time they were given regular cosmetic treatments and soaked in oils and perfumes. When they finally got their opportunity, they only had one chance to impress King Ahasuerus. Unless he subsequently asked for them by name, it was a one-night stand. If they did not "delight him," they would not be called back. Ahasuerus, the king of Persia, essentially held a lavish beauty pageant with a twist, inviting women from all over the kingdom to compete for the coveted title of Queen of Persia. Had television been around in those days, this would have made an absorbing and popular reality show.

As for Esther, her wise uncle, Mordecai, counseled her to conceal her Jewish heritage and participate in the contest. It was a great opportunity, albeit one with definite risk, given the king's antipathy for Jews. So it was that in the palace, Esther faced numerous challenges and temptations, but was also careful to heed her uncle's advice. Esther went from living the life of a slave, or rather poverty, to that of royalty. She had access to the finest beautifying products and food that was meant for royalty. How would she balance the many temptations presented to her while still remaining grounded in her true identity? Mordecai stayed close, *"walk[ing] around in front of the court of the harem [every day], to learn how Esther was and how she fared"* (Esther 2:11).

Despite the difficulties and the danger, Esther remained steadfast in her faith. One wonders whether she ever questioned Mordecai's advice or if she ever felt guilty because of the deceit she was practicing. Irrespective of how she felt, she stayed the course, trusting God that everything would go well. And it did. Esther's humility and grace set her apart from the other contestants, and she won the favor of the king. He loved Esther more than all the other women, and of all the virgins, she won his devotion. He set the royal crown on her head and made her queen instead of Vashti.

Remember that it was via deception that Esther initially entered the palace and was able to stay there. She kept her secret for a long time. We are often told to be bold and outspoken in our faith, but Esther's example teaches us there may also be times when we should stay under the radar, at least until the time is right.

However, Esther's true purpose in the palace was yet to be revealed. The king promoted Haman, one of his officials, and "*set his seat above all the officials who were with him*," making him the second in command (Esther 3:1). Haman was a wicked advisor to the king and harbored a deep hatred for the Jews. He was a descendant of Agag, king of the Amalekites, who were ancient enemies of God's people (Numbers 24:7; 1 Samuel 15:8).

Mordecai added fuel to the fire of Haman's anti-Semitism by refusing to bow to him when he passed through the palace courts each day. Infuriated by Mordecai's disobedience and disrespect, Haman nevertheless felt it beneath him to lay hands on Mordecai. Having discovered that Mordecai was a Jew, Haman saw a golden opportunity to kill two birds with one stone. He would punish the individual who slighted him and strike a blow against the Jews. He devised a plan to annihilate them. He cast the lot, called "pur," to determine the day that the Jews would be exterminated (Esther 3:7–9). The Feast of Purim, still celebrated by Jews today, commemorates the Jews' deliverance from Haman's plot (Esther 9:20–32).

Mordecai, who had become a trusted servant in the palace, discovered the plot and urgently sought Esther's help. He wanted her to go before the king and present to him the details of Haman's evil plan. She replied, via a messenger, that it was not a simple thing for her to go before the king. Everyone in the place knew:

> *"That if any man or woman goes to the king*
> *inside the inner court without being called, there is*
> *but one law—all alike are to be put to death."*
> —Esther 4:11

Esther shared her concerns that she had not been summoned to see Ahasuerus for the last thirty days. Esther faced a daunting decision. She could remain silent, preserve her own safety, or risk everything to save her people. In a moment of profound courage, Esther resolved to approach the king, uninvited, to plead for the lives of her fellow Jews. The danger was obvious. Not only would she be breaking palace protocol, but, assuming the king didn't have her dragged away and executed without listening to her, she would also be revealing her deception.

To help Esther decide, Mordecai warned her that she too would die if Haman's planned extermination went ahead.

> *"'Do not think that in the king's palace you will escape*
> *any more than all the other Jews. For if you keep silence at such*
> *a time as this, relief and deliverance will rise for the Jews*
> *from another quarter, but you and your father's family*
> *will perish. Who knows? Perhaps you have come*
> *to royal dignity for just such a time as this.'"*
> —Esther 4:13–14

Esther agreed to approach the king, finishing her message to her uncle with the ominous words, *"I will go to the king, though it is against the law, and if I perish, I perish"* (Esther 4:16). Then gathering her strength, Esther fasted and prayed for three days, seeking God's guidance and protection. The Jews of the kingdom, having all been advised through word of mouth what was happening, also prayed and fasted for Esther, who they must have felt certain had been elevated to the Crown to be the agent of God's salvation. Here we see the value of a community of believers. Consider how much confidence Esther would have gained for her difficult assignment by knowing that so many were praying and fasting with her. The psalmist wrote that God commands a blessing where there is unity (Psalm 133).

> *"On the third day Esther put on her royal robes and stood in the inner court of the king's palace, opposite the king's hall. The king was sitting on his royal throne inside the palace opposite the entrance to the palace. As soon as the king saw Queen Esther standing in the court, she won his favor and he held out to her the golden scepter that was in his hand. Then Esther approached and touched the top of the scepter. The king said to her, 'What is it, Queen Esther? What is your request? It shall be given you, even to the half of my kingdom.' Then Esther said, 'If it pleases the king, let the king and Haman come today to a banquet that I have prepared for the king.'"*
> —Esther 5:1–4

In Esther 5:1–4, we see Queen Esther ready to take a significant risk to save her people. After fasting and likely engaging in deep prayer and meditation for three days, she is prepared to implement her plan. Esther has contemplated all possible scenarios and their consequences, unable to share or discuss her thoughts with anyone else but God.

She has already accepted the potential cost of her life, as expressed in her words in Esther 4:16, "*If I perish, I perish.*" Esther's preparation involved dressing in her royal robes, a testament to her readiness to present herself before King Ahasuerus. This act would undoubtedly have brought on a potent emotional response, yet it was crucial for her to maintain her composure. It is likely that she felt a deep sense of apprehension and a surge of adrenaline, leading to increased heart rate, elevated blood pressure, and other physiological responses typically associated with high-stress situations. A key aspect of training for an agent or undercover agent is the ability to maintain a calm and composed demeanor in critical situations. This allows the best possible mental acuity, allowing an agent to make clear decisions.

Once prepared, Esther positions herself in the inner court of the king's palace, opposite the king's hall, in a bid to attract his attention. Cloaked in the armor of her faith, she is called by the king, and as she approaches his throne, her heart pounds with trepidation. To her relief, the king extends his golden scepter, granting her permission to speak.

Esther's willingness to step out of her comfort zone and take risks for the greater good inspires us to confront injustice and stand up for what is right. In a society where complacency often prevails, Esther's example reminds us that our actions, no matter how small, can make a significant impact on the lives of others.

Esther did not immediately reveal Haman's wicked plot. At this critical juncture, Esther possessed the opportunity to request anything she desired, and the king would undoubtedly fulfill her wish. Based on Esther's commanding presence and unwavering self-confidence, it is plausible to assume that the king held her in high regard and found her alluring in ways that some of his other wives may not have exuded.

Esther adopted an entirely distinct approach, setting herself apart from the others. It appears that the king placed great value on strength and confidence, qualities that Esther personified.

Esther asked that Haman be invited to dine with her and the king. Verse 6 says while they were drinking wine, the king repeated his earlier words to Esther regarding her petition, but Esther demurred and asked for a second feast to be held the following day. Esther was very cleverly setting Haman up—you might say she was buttering him up—by making him feel even more important than he already did about himself. After eating with the king and queen, Haman boasted of this special favor bestowed upon him (Esther 5:12). Lulled into a false sense of security and overwhelmed with self-importance, Haman nevertheless was still irritated by Mordecai, and he planned to kill him.

Once again as they were drinking wine at the second feast, the king asked Esther what she wanted. In an eloquent and gracefully presented petition, Esther revealed Haman's plot and implored the king to spare her people. This was the first time she confessed her heritage. In Esther 7:4 she said, *"For we have been sold, I and my people, to be destroyed, to be killed, and to be annihilated."* The king, unaware of the danger that had loomed over his beloved queen, was filled with righteous anger. Haman's treachery was exposed, and the king showed him no mercy, ordering his immediate execution—a just and swift punishment for his crimes.

Esther's bravery, intelligence, beauty, and unwavering faith saved her people from destruction. The Jewish community rejoiced, celebrating their deliverance from the hands of their enemies. Mordecai, recognizing Esther's pivotal role in their salvation, proclaimed a yearly festival called Purim to commemorate their deliverance and to remind future generations of the power of faith and courage.

Despite her fear, Esther hid her Jewish heritage, essentially practicing a deliberate deception, and when asked to by Mordecai, she approached the king and was able to unveil the plot against the Jews. Often people will refer to Esther's decision to hide her Jewish identity as a sin. But Mordecai had told Esther in Esther 2:10 not to reveal her identity; he understood that if her true identity was revealed, she may have been kicked out of the palace. Mordecai understood the inner workings of the palace and understood Persian culture much better. Essentially, Mordecai was Esther's "handler"—a common term when an agent is working in an undercover capacity. The handler also maintains close contact and provides useful information to the agent, which, in this case, Esther was able to utilize properly. So it was not a sin for Esther to hide her identity since God had placed her at that place for the exact purpose that was meant for her.

Neither Esther nor Mordecai were perfect people, but they were faithful people and God chose them.

> *"For Mordecai the Jew was next in rank to King Ahasuerus, and he was powerful among the Jews and popular with his many kindred, for he sought the good of his people and interceded for the welfare of all his descendants."*
> —ESTHER 10:3

Esther's story resonates deeply in today's world, where challenges and injustices abound. Her life teaches us valuable lessons that we can apply to our own lives in modern times. Esther's unwavering faith in God serves as a reminder that even in the face of adversity, we can find strength and courage through our relationship with the divine. In a world filled with uncertainty, Esther's story encourages us to trust in God's plan and seek His guidance in all aspects of our lives. Esther's humility and grace remind us of the importance of inner beauty and character. Her outer beauty was just as important and should not be dismissed, but in a world that often values external appearances and superficiality, Esther's story encourages us to cultivate qualities such as kindness, compassion, and integrity, which have the power to transform lives and bring about positive change.

CONCLUSION

MESSAGE OF HOPE IN TIMES OF UNCERTAINTY

There are many individuals in the Bible, like Ruth and Boaz, who may not have had any flaws identified in their stories; however, it does not mean that they did not possess any. The book of Ruth, only four chapters long, tells a beautiful tale of redemption, faithfulness, and love. Living in Moab, Mahlon and Chilion married Moabite women, Orpah and Ruth. Tragedy struck this family when their father, Elimelech, died, leaving their mother, Naomi, a widow. Time passed, and both Mahlon and Chilion also died, leaving their wives childless and widowed. Naomi, burdened by grief and loss, decided to return to her homeland, Bethlehem. She urged her daughters-in-law to stay in Moab and find new husbands among their own people. Orpah tearfully bid farewell to Naomi and returned to her family, but Ruth clung to her mother-in-law, refusing to leave her side. She said, in a voice filled with determination and loyalty, *"Where you go, I will go; where you lodge, I will lodge; your people shall be my people, and your God my God"* (Ruth 1:16). Naomi, moved by Ruth's devotion, accepted her as a daughter and they journeyed together to Bethlehem.

We may not know a whole lot about Ruth's background or her family upbringing, but we can make a reasonable assumption, based on the way Naomi loved her sons, that she would have only chosen the best women available to marry them—women of higher status or potentially well-off families. Ruth's act of devotion to Naomi may have been a part of her upbringing—the way she was raised—but it also may have been a genuine reflection of her personality. Whatever motivated her to stay with Naomi given the potential dangers they would face as two women traveling by themselves, unprotected, we know God's hand was on her life. With the benefit of hindsight, we can easily see how God works all things together for good. However, neither Naomi nor Ruth had such an advantage.

The grieving widow and her foreign daughter-in-law, also widowed, arrived in Bethlehem at the beginning of harvest time, facing a life of uncertainty and hardship. As widows, they were vulnerable and relied on the kindness of others for survival. Ruth, with a heart full of love and a desire to provide for her mother-in-law, took it upon herself to glean in the fields, gathering leftover grain after the harvesters. Ruth's unwavering loyalty and devotion to Naomi exemplify the importance of selflessness and sacrificial love. In a world that often prioritizes individualism and self-interest, Ruth's story reminds us of the power of compassion and the impact it can have on the lives of others.

When Ruth came to Boaz's field, he told her to take as much as she needed, and promised that the young men working would leave her in peace. Furthermore, he fed her and protected her as she gathered food to support herself and Naomi. Eventually Ruth and Boaz were married. Boaz's kindness and generosity toward Ruth demonstrate the importance of using our resources and influence to uplift and support those in need. Boaz's actions serve as a reminder that we can make a difference in the lives of others, no matter our social status or position. Ruth and Boaz highlight the significance of God's providence and faithfulness. Despite the hardships and uncertainties they faced, God orchestrated their paths and brought about a beautiful redemption. Their story encourages us to trust in God's plan, even when life seems uncertain or challenging. Ruth and Boaz emphasize the value of inclusivity and acceptance. Ruth, a Moabite woman, was welcomed into the community of Bethlehem and became an integral part of God's redemptive plan. Their story challenges us to embrace diversity and extend love and hospitality to those who may be different from us.

It was Ruth's and Boaz's characteristics and behaviors that were eventually passed down to their descendants. We often fail to consider that Ruth's story of resilience began with the loss of her husband, her brother-in-law, her father-in-law, and ultimately her home. God used a grieving mother and a widow to set the stage for what unfolds in the New Testament, ensuring that there would be purpose in their pain. Ruth and Boaz had a son named Obed, who had a son named Jesse, who fathered King David, who ultimately fathered King Solomon. However, it was some of their flaws and the fact that they were chosen that took those men down paths they ultimately ended up on. If it wasn't for King David's flaws, he most likely would not have fathered Solomon. God was able to use David's flaws to bless him and his descendants. Eventually, it was through Ruth and Boaz's lineage that Jesus Christ was brought into this world. Boaz was known as the "Kinsman Redeemer" in the book of Ruth. However, the Perfect Redeemer would not be born for another 1140 years.

In reading the Bible, a book that is riddled with many flawed people, one is constantly reminded of times to believe and have blind faith in God. This idea can be very difficult to articulate to someone who may not be a true believer or one who may question the existence of God. In a world where chaos and sadness seem to prevail, the narrative of Ruth and Boaz serves as a reminder that good-hearted individuals still exist. It is disheartening to witness how many discussions within our society commence with defensiveness, leading to division. Amidst Ruth's crumbling life, God's intervention brought Boaz into her story. While we may not have noticed any flaws in these characters, their existence cannot be denied. This tale serves as a reminder that goodness persists in this world, even when it might not always feel that way.

The reality is that we are all flawed in many ways. We are in no way perfect, and the only One who was perfect was crucified unjustly for being perfect so that our flaws could be forgiven. I would be remiss if I did not end this book with a message of hopefulness rather than one of discouragement. When I first began this journey, it was an opportunity for self-reflection and self-healing because of some unfortunate decisions I made and the flaws I possess. At times, I felt I wasn't worthy of living a life of joy and peace, or even of being loved, simply because of the mistakes I had made or the people I had hurt along the way.

Finding the proper closing for this book was not an easy task. I drew my final thoughts from an event that is rarely spoken of or written about, but one that will provide context around how we are all flawed and can still be chosen. The specific moment takes place in the New Testament of the Bible in Matthew 17. In this chapter, it is known as the Transfiguration of Jesus.

"Six days later, Jesus took with him Peter and James and his brother John and led them up a high mountain, by themselves. And he was transfigured before them, and his face shone

> *like the sun, and his clothes became dazzling white. Suddenly there appeared to them Moses and Elijah, talking with him. Then Peter said to Jesus, 'Lord, it is good for us to be here; if you wish, I will make three dwellings here, one for you, one for Moses, and one for Elijah.' While he was still speaking, suddenly a bright cloud overshadowed them, and from the cloud a voice said, 'This is my Son, the Beloved; with him I am well pleased; listen to him!' When the disciples heard this, they fell to the ground and were overcome by fear. But Jesus came and touched them, saying, 'Get up and do not be afraid.' And when they looked up, they saw no one except Jesus himself alone."*
>
> —MATTHEW 17:1–8

The story of Jesus' Transfiguration holds profound significance, yet it is often overlooked. I pose the question: why did God choose Moses and Elijah to speak with Jesus during this transformative moment? God could have selected countless individuals from the Old Testament to witness Jesus' glory. Traditionally, it has been suggested that Moses' and Elijah's presence served to validate Jesus' divinity to his disciples, enabling them to spread the word about their encounter.

However, I propose an alternative perspective: examining the story from the viewpoint of Moses and Elijah. In previous chapters, we learned that God took both Moses and Elijah to Heaven. Moses, despite his advanced age of 120, remained in good health. Both men had fasted for forty days, and God was present when they left Earth. During their lives on Earth, Moses and Elijah communicated with God regularly. However, they also experienced significant challenges and low points. Elijah faced intense fear and anxiety due to Jezebel's threats, leading to thoughts of suicide. Moses was heartbroken and discouraged when he was denied entry to the Promised Land despite his faithful service. In light of these challenges, I believe God brought Moses and Elijah back to see Jesus in His glory as a testament to their unwavering faith, love, and dedication to serving Him. Despite their human flaws, God chose them to play a crucial role in His ultimate plan of salvation for humanity.

Even in their darkest moments, Moses and Elijah could not have imagined how their service would ultimately be used in God's plan. Their presence at Jesus' Transfiguration atop Mount Tabor near Galilee symbolizes God's message to us: Although we may not fully comprehend His ways now, someday we too will have the opportunity to witness His glory and communicate with Him as Moses and Elijah did.

As I turn the final page of this profound journey of self-transformation, I am filled with a deep desire to glean wisdom from my past experiences in order to pave the way for a brighter future. Throughout different phases of my life, I have savored moments of joy, yet in recent years, the shadows of negativity seemed to overshadow the light. Peace eluded me, and I struggled to be fully present for my loved ones; I was consumed by thoughts of where I should be instead of embracing the present moment. My sole sense of purpose seemed rooted in work, and I yearned for balance to prove my worth to others. Quick to anger and lacking patience, I realized that true happiness had become a distant memory.

The concept of happiness felt like a fleeting emotion, overshadowed by the daily roller coaster of feelings. Although I craved an escape, I remained unsure of where that escape truly led. I discovered solace in fixing others' problems, avoiding my own in the process.

When I began writing this book in February 2023, I swiftly penned the initial three chapters within weeks. Yet, as I finished the third chapter, a cruel twist of fate hit home when I found my own house flooded during a storm, mirroring Noah's tale in an unexpected way. Despite this setback, I persevered and completed two more chapters, only to wake up one Sunday to news of my daughter's accident, involving two cars—both mine. Each week brought fresh challenges, tempting me to abandon this project. Work pressures mounted, and unwarranted scrutiny tested my resolve. Still, I soldiered on, determined to finish what I started.

My children, observing my struggle, urged me to see this book through to the end. I cannot explain how I endured, except to credit the Holy Spirit for guiding each step. I am grateful for a forgiving God who chose me despite my flaws and myriad challenges.

The message here is one of acceptance and love from a higher being who created each individual fearfully and wonderfully. Despite self-doubt or feelings of unworthiness, it is emphasized that one is chosen and acceptable in the eyes of God. *Chosen and Flawed* was written to encourage us to move away from negative self-talk or behaviors that hinder personal growth and service in God's Kingdom. It stresses the importance of acknowledging your gifts and not disqualifying yourself due to various struggles or challenges. It is a reminder that living a life of mediocrity by making excuses only deprives you of the greatness God has called you for.

Through Jesus, the promise of an abundant life is extended to those who choose to walk alongside Him. This promise includes the assurance of redemption and a pathway to the presence of God. The sacrifice of Jesus is emphasized as the bridge that surpasses barriers and allows for a confident and direct approach to the Almighty.

Additionally, it is important to recognize that even those who are entrusted with conveying the teachings of God can be fallible due to personal biases and beliefs. This serves as a reminder that no human is without flaws, and yet God values and loves each and every one of us. Our flaws, no matter how significant, have been fully paid for by the man who was crucified on a wooden cross, which is a reminder of the very tree from which the original sin originated.

This reflection urges us to embrace the grace and forgiveness offered through Jesus' sacrifice. It reminds us that our flaws do not define our worth in the eyes of God, and that we are all deserving of His love and salvation.

Amen.

ACKNOWLEDGMENTS

In recognition of their patience, I express my deepest gratitude to Pamela, Destiny, Elisabeth, Emma, Ethan, and Levi who provided me with the grace I needed to heal during the process of writing this book.

I would like to acknowledge David Cairns' invaluable assistance during the early stages of character development. His guidance helped keep me on track, especially when I strayed from the intended path, which occurred frequently.

The Scribe team deserves special recognition for their contributions: Ellie Cole, whose exceptional project management skills were instrumental in bringing this book to life; Anna Dorfman, whose artistic vision perfectly captured my concept for the cover; and Holly Gorman, whose insightful questions inspired me to think critically and deepen my analysis. Your support was essential in completing this project.

Finally, I extend my heartfelt appreciation to Sienna and Emmett for helping me comprehend true grief and enabling me to properly grieve my own past.

ABOUT THE AUTHOR

ARVINDER "VINNY" GINDA is a co-owner of Emotional Intelligence, LLC, where he leads workshops on critical decision-making, offers leadership courses, and provides education on how technology affects the developing brain. His ten years as a local law enforcement officer and two-decade career as an FBI Special Agent, focused on international and domestic terrorism programs, hostage negotiations, various overseas deployments, and high-profile interrogations, have given him a unique perspective on human behavior. He holds a degree in psychology from California State University, Sacramento. Originally from India, Arvinder moved to Northern California with his family and has since made it their home.

www.ingramcontent.com/pod-product-compliance
Lightning Source LLC
Chambersburg PA
CBHW060518080526
44586CB00012B/534